THE BIBLE-BELIEVER'S GUIDE TO
BAPTIST DISTINCTIVES
VOLUME ONE

Biblical Authority

Autonomy of Churches

Priesthood of the Believer

---

by Linton M. Smith Jr.
Th.B., Th.M., D.D.

© Copyright 2009 by Linton M. Smith Jr.

All Scripture quotations are from
the King James 1611
Authorized Version of the Bible

DayStar
Publishing
P.O. Box 464
Miamitown, OH 45041

TABLE OF CONTENTS

About the Holy Bible, J. Sidlow Baxter wrote

"THIS IS THE GREATEST BOOK ON EARTH,
"UNPARALLELED IT STANDS;
"ITS AUTHOR GOD, ITS TRUTH DIVINE
"INSPIRED IN EVERY WORD AND LINE,
"THO' WRIT' BY HUMAN HANDS.

"THIS IS THE LIVING ROCK OF TRUTH
"WHICH ALL ASSAULTS DEFIES,
"O'ER EVERY STORMY BLAST OF TIME
"IT TOWERS WITH MAJESTY SUBLIME;
"IT LIVES, AND NEVER DIES.

"THIS IS THE VOLUME OF THE CROSS;
"ITS SAVING TRUTH IS SURE;
"ITS DOCTRINE PURE, ITS HISTORY TRUE,
"ITS GOSPEL OLD, YET EVER NEW,
"SHALL EVERMORE ENDURE." [1]

---

[1] **J. Sidlow Baxter**, Explore the Book, p. 13

PART ONE

BIBLICAL AUTHORITY
OF THE BELIEVER

<u>Asked about his salvation, Martin Luther replied</u>

"Do you FEEL that you have been forgiven?" "He answered: "No; but I am as SURE, as there is a God in Heaven!

<u>No doubt with that same thought in mind Luther wrote</u>

"For feelings come and feelings go,
'And feelings are deceiving.
'My warrant is the word of God;
'Naught else is worth believing.

"Though all my heart should feel condemned
'For want of some sweet token,
'There is One greater than my heart
'Whose word cannot be broken.

'I'll trust in God's unchanging word
'Till soul and body sever;
"For though all things shall pass away,
'HIS WORD SHALL STAND FOREVER."

PREFACE

Like a "punch-drunk"[2] boxer who comes out swinging every time he hears a bell, Baptists seem intent on infighting. Nonetheless, Baptists are the first to step to the forefront of any battle in defense of the faith. Having fought every heresy that ever came along, we are now divided among ourselves to fight over issues that should have been settled long ago. Maybe it is because most of us have never had to labor in the shadow of the antichrist Roman Catholic church, that we fail to see what the final battle is all about. Many no longer see any point in calling themselves "Baptist" or defending those distinctive beliefs that have made us hated by Catholics and Protestants alike. Because the lines have been so blurred, we have all the more reason to firmly establish what we really believe. A dozen different groups claim to be "true" Baptists— that is "their" problem. My primary concern is to be a "true" CHRISTIAN and next to *"earnestly contend for the faith which was once delivered unto the saints"* (Jude 1:3). Doing that is what made me a Baptist.

After the Lord brought me out of the Charismatic movement, I began to study the Bible for myself. I determined not to hold any doctrine too precious that I would not give it up if the Bible taught otherwise. After a few years, I took stock— studying the Bible had made me a Baptist. Through the years I have stood for those same truths I learned back then.

It is lamentable that those who love the truth must often stand alone today. However, because of the extent of our knowledge of Bible doctrine, as Bible-believers we, more than any preceding generation, are responsible for propagating the truth we hold dear.

---

[2] **punch-drunk** 1. Showing signs of brain damage caused by repeated blows to the head. Used especially of a boxer. 2. Behaving in a bewildered, confused, or dazed manner. American Heritage Dictionary

As Jeremiah proclaimed, God's people today *are not valiant for the truth.* But, we never stand alone when we stand for Him. Therefore, let us take our stand and teach the truth that it die not with us.

<u>Scripture encourages us in this regard</u>

> "And others had trial of cruel mockings and scourgings, yea, moreover of bonds and imprisonment:
>
> "They were stoned, they were sawn asunder, were tempted, were slain with the sword: they wandered about in sheepskins and goatskins; being destitute, afflicted, tormented;
>
> "(Of whom the world was not worthy:) they wandered in deserts, and in mountains, and in dens and caves of the earth.
>
> "And these all, having obtained a good report through faith, received not the promise:
>
> "God having provided some better thing for us, that they without us should not be made perfect.
>
> "Wherefore seeing we also are compassed about with so great a cloud of witnesses, let us lay aside every weight, and the sin which doth so easily beset us, and let us run with patience the race that is set before us,
>
> "Looking unto Jesus the author and finisher of our faith; who for the joy that was set before him endured the cross, despising the shame, and is set down at the right hand of the throne of God."
>
> — Hebrews 11:36-12:2

This scripture brings to mind the following familiar hymn and story. This hymn has often been a blessing to me and I include it here for your edification as well.

SO SEND I YOU

by Margaret Clarkson

"'So send I you to labor unrewarded,
To serve unpaid, unloved, unsought, unknown,
To bear rebuke, to suffer scorn and scoffing,
So send I you to toil for me alone.

"So send I you to bind the bruised and broken,
O'er wand'ring souls to work, to weep, to wake,
To bear the burdens of a world aweary—
So send I you to suffer for My sake.

"So send I you— to loneliness and longing,
With heart a-hungering for the loved and known;
Forsaking home and kindred, friend and dear one,
So send I you— to know my love alone.

"So send I you— to leave your life's ambitions,
To die to dear desire, self-will resign,
To labor long and love where men revile you,
So send I you— to lose your life in mine.

"So send I you to hearts made hard by hatred,
To eyes made blind because they will not see,
To spend, tho' it be blood, to spend and spare not—
So send I you to taste of Calvary.'

"The text of 'So Send I You,' sometimes called *'the finest missionary hymn of the twentieth century,'* was written by a young Canadian, then just 22. Born in Saskatchewan,

Margaret Clarkson grew up from age five in Toronto, graduating as a teacher in 1935. Jobs were so scarce that she had to spend seven years in the far north of Ontario, first in a lumber camp, then in a gold-mining area, before returning to teach her remaining 31 years in Toronto, retiring in 1973.

"For over 50 years she has been known for her poems and articles in Christian periodicals, for her many hymns, and for her books...

"Of the writing of this text Miss Clarkson has written:

"In the north I experienced deep loneliness of every kind; mental, cultural and particularly, spiritual— I found no Bible-teaching church fellowship, and only one or two isolated Christians, in those years.

"Studying the Word one night and thinking of the loneliness of my situation, I came to John 20, and the words 'So send I you.' Because of a physical disability I could never go to the mission field, but God seemed to tell me that night that this was my mission field, and this was where He had sent me. I had written verse all my life, so it was natural for me to express my thoughts in a poem."[3]

God never called us to a life of ease, but to bear a cross. As He was persecuted, so we may expect to be persecuted, as well. Yet through our sufferings in the name of our Saviour we become a sweet savor unto our Lord and we may count it all joy when we are privileged to experience those sufferings.

The apostle Paul wrote unto the church at Corinth

"Now thanks be unto God, which always causeth us to triumph in Christ, and maketh manifest THE SAVOUR OF HIS KNOWLEDGE by us in every place.

"For we are unto God A SWEET SAVOUR OF CHRIST, in them that are saved, and in them that perish:

"To the one we are THE SAVOUR OF DEATH unto death; and to the other THE SAVOUR OF LIFE unto life. And who is sufficient for these things?"

---

[3] *Wheaton College Archives,* www.wheaton.edu/learnres/ARCSC/exhibits/

"**For we are not as many, which corrupt the word of God: but as of sincerity, but as of God, in the sight of God speak we in Christ.**"
— II Corinthians 2:14-17

But, the knowledge which is a sweet savour unto the Lord (vs. 15) and unto the child of God (**"them that are saved"**), is a stench in the nostrils of the world, the flesh and the devil (**"them that perish"**). Notice in verse fourteen, that being a sweet savour has to do with **"knowledge"** and in verse seventeen, with **"many, which corrupt the word of God."** So, it is vitally important that we have and preach the right knowledge of the word of God **"in every place."**

In the preface to his book The Lord's Table, Andrew Murray wrote the following words of wisdom and guidance for his readers and students of the word of God.

"On the use of this little volume I would fain say two things which lie upon my heart.

"The first is this: that the Christian who desires to make use of it must not be content merely to read and to understand the portion for the day, but must take time to meditate upon it and to appropriate it. I am convinced that one chief cause why some do not grow more in grace is that they do not take time to hold converse with the Lord in secret. Spiritual, divine truth does not thus become our possession at once. Although I understand what I read, although I consent heartily to it, although I receive it, it may speedily fade away and be forgotten, unless by private meditation I give it time to become fixed and rooted in me, to become united and identified with me. Christians, give yourselves, give your Lord time to transfer His heavenly thoughts to your inner, spiritual life. When you have read a portion, set yourselves in silence before God. Take time to remain before Him until He has made His word living and powerful in your souls. Then does it become the life and the power of your life.

"And this brings me to the second remark which I desire to make. It is this: that the Christian must take special care that he do not suffer himself to be led away from the Word of God by the many manuals which in our days are seeing the light. These books will have this result, —whenever a man seeks his instruction only in what the writer has to say, he then becomes accustomed to take everything at second hand. These books can become a blessing to the reader only when they bring him always to that portion of God's Word which is treated of in order that he may meditate further upon it himself as from the mouth of God. Christians, there is in the Word of God an incredible power. The blessing which lies hid in it is inconceivable. See to it that when you have read a portion you always return to that passage of the Scriptures of which an explanation is given. Receive that not as the word of man, but, as it is in truth, the Word of God, which works mightily in those that believe. Hold fellowship with God through the Word. Take time to speak with Him about it, to give an answer to Him concerning it. Then shall you understand what the Lord Jesus says: "The words which I speak unto you, they are spirit and life." Then shall Word and sacrament gloriously work together, to make you increase in prayer and in the life of God.

"That the Eternal God may bless this little volume also, to make His children learn His own Word, is the prayer of the author for all his readers." [4]

If you have a sincere desire to know God and understand His word in a deeper way, some of the basics are in this book. Seek not only to learn doctrine, but to experience God and receive instruction from the Holy Spirit and you will not be disappointed.

We will now look at those biblical principals and practices that distinguish Baptists from Catholics, Protestants and all cults.

---

[4] **Andrew Murray**, The Lord's Table — A Help to the Right Observance of the Holy Supper, (Fleming H. Revell Company) Copyright 1897

INTRODUCTION

The letters that form the word "B-A-P-T-I-S-T-S" each stand for a particular belief. This set of beliefs are commonly referred to as the "Baptist Distinctives." These eight distinctive doctrines are the core of the basic doctrines believed by all Baptists. While not designed that way, these doctrines set in order, make up the acrostic[5] "B-A-P-T-I-S-T-S."

B

Biblical Authority

The Bible is the final authority in all matters of belief and practice, because the Bible is inspired by God and bears the absolute authority of God Himself. Whatever the Bible affirms, Baptists accept as true. No human opinion or decree of any church group can override the Bible. Even creeds and confessions of faith, which attempt to articulate the theology of Scripture, do not carry Scripture's inherent authority.

II Timothy 3:15-17; I Thessalonians 2:13; II Peter 1:20-21

---

[5] **acrostic,** n. 1. A poem or series of lines in which certain letters, usually the first in each line, form a name, motto, or message when read in sequence. <u>American Heritage Dictionary</u>

A

Autonomy of the Local Church

The local Baptist church is an independent body accountable to the Lord Jesus Christ, the head of the church. All human authority for governing the local church resides within the local church itself. Thus the church is autonomous, or self-governing. No religious hierarchy outside the local church may dictate a church's beliefs or practices. Autonomy does not mean isolation. An independent Baptist church may fellowship with other churches around mutual interests and in an associational tie, but an independent Baptist church shall not come under the authority of any other body.
Colossians 1:18; II Corinthians 8:1-5, 19, 23

P

Priesthood of the Believer

"Priest" is defined as "one authorized to perform the sacred rites of a religion, especially as a mediatory agent between man and God." Every believer today is a priest of God and may enter into His presence in prayer directly through our Great High Priest, Jesus Christ. No other mediator is needed between God and people. As priests, we can study God's Word, pray for others, and offer spiritual worship to God. We all have equal access to God— whether we are a preacher or not.
I Peter 2:5, 9; Revelation 5:9-10

T

Two Ordinances

The local church should practice two ordinances:
1. Baptism of **believers** (not unbelievers or infants) by immersion in water, identifying the individual with Christ in His death, burial, and resurrection, and
2. The Lord's Supper, or communion, commemorating His death for our sins.

Matthew 28:19, 20; I Corinthians 11:23-32

I

Individual Soul Liberty

Every individual, whether a believer or an unbeliever, has the liberty to choose what he believes is right in the religious realm. No one should be forced to assent to any belief against his will. Baptists have always opposed religious persecution. However, this liberty does not exempt one from responsibility to the Word of God or from accountability to God Himself.
Romans 14:5, 12; II Corinthians 4:2; Titus 1:9

S

Saved, Baptized Church Membership

Local independent Baptist church membership is restricted to individuals who give a believable testimony of personal faith in Christ and have publicly identified themselves with Him in believer's baptism. All the members of a local independent Baptist church who are believers can, therefore, experience an atmosphere of oneness in Christ, wherein they can endeavor to "keep the unity of the Spirit in the bond of peace."
Acts 2:41-47; I Corinthians 12:12; II Corinthians 6:14; Ephesians 4:3

Two Offices

T The Bible mandates only two offices in the church—bishop and deacon. These two offices exist *within* the local independent Baptist church, not as a hierarchy outside or over it.

Separation of Church and State

S God established both the church and the civil government, and He gave each its own distinct sphere of operation. The government's purposes are outlined in Romans 13:1-7 and the church's purposes in Matthew 28:19-20. Neither should control the other, nor should there be an alliance between the two. Christians in a free society can properly influence government toward righteousness, which is not the same as a denomination or group of churches controlling the government.
Matthew 22:15-22; Acts 15:17-29

THE ONE BOOK

Yes, Yes, THAT'S THE ONE!

WORD OF GOD

Abell

FOR SUCH A TIME AS THIS

Independent Baptists arrived at these distinctives through careful study of the Bible. That is why these teachings might more precisely be called "Biblical distinctives of Baptists" rather than "Baptist distinctives." These teachings emerged as Baptist distinctives because individual Baptist churches have consistently and independently held to them, not because some group of Baptist leaders composed the list and then imposed the distinctives on local churches. Church groups other than Baptists have held some of these Baptist beliefs, and one may even find churches that hold all of the distinctives, although they do not even call themselves "Baptist." Such groups are "baptistic," but for some reason they choose not to be identified as Baptists. On the other hand, some churches calling themselves "Baptist" are not truly Baptist, because they no longer hold the historic Baptist beliefs or even the fundamentals of the Christian faith.

Baptists are people of "the Book" above everything else. And Baptists enjoy a priceless heritage of generations who have exalted God's Son, our Saviour, and have proclaimed God's inspired Word.

I pray you will be blessed in studying the biblical "Baptist distinctives" of Bible-believers that I have laid out in this book.

This Bible contains the mind of God,
the state of man, the way of salvation,
the doom of sinners and the happiness of believers.

Its doctrines are holy, its precepts are binding,
its histories are true, and its decisions are immutable.

Read it to be wise, believe it to be safe,
and practice it to be holy.

It contains light to direct you,
food to support you, and comfort to cheer you.

It is the traveler's map, the pilgrim's staff,
the pilot's compass, the soldier's sword
and the Christian's character.

Here Paradise is restored, Heaven opened,
and the gates of Hell disclosed.

Christ is its grand object, our good is its design,
and the glory of God its end.

It should fill the memory, rule the heart,
and guide the feet.

Read it slowly, frequently, and prayerfully.

It is given you in life and will be opened
in the judgment and will be remembered forever.

It involves the highest responsibility,
will reward the greatest labour,
and will condemn all who trifle with its sacred contents

THE KEY TO DOCTRINAL INTEGRITY

The nineteenth century French theologian, Louis Gaussen, put it plainly

> "It follows from all we have said, that there are in the Christian world but two schools, or TWO RELIGIONS: that which puts the Bible above everything, and that which puts something above the Bible."[6]

Let others believe what they may, but as Bible-believing independent Baptists, we respectfully put the King James Bible above every thing. It is sad that we must distinguish ourselves as "Bible-believing" Baptists, but today not even all Baptists claim to believe that the Bible they hold in their hands is, indeed, the inspired word of God.

The American Heritage Dictionary defines "authority" as

> "The right and power to govern or judge…"[7]

Everything we know about God comes from **one book**, the Bible. It must be the **final authority** in all matters of faith and practice. Therefore, **biblical authority** is at the root of all other doctrines, because what we believe about "the book" determines how authoritative it is to us in matters of doctrine. Unfortunately, in the midst of the current quagmire of more than 200 different Bible versions, we must clarify what we mean when we say "the Bible." "Biblical authority" means little, unless we have an "authoritative Bible." Just where can God's word be found and how reliable is it? For us, the answer is simple. The only "Bible" we know, is the *King James 1611 Authorized Version*. It has never led us astray, and why should we forsake it now?

---

[6] **Louis Gaussen**, Theopneustia: The Plenary Inspiration of the Holy Scriptures

[7] American Heritage Talking Dictionary

John Dryden wrote of the origin of the Bible

"Whence but from Heaven, could men unskilled in arts,

"In several ages born, in several parts,

"Weave such agreeing truths? Or how, or why,

"Should all conspire to cheat us with a lie!

"Unasked their pains, ungrateful their advice,

"Starving their gain, and martyrdom their price."

— John Dryden [8]

King David, the Psalmist of Israel, wrote

"I will worship toward thy holy temple, and praise thy name for thy lovingkindness and for thy TRUTH: for thou hast magnified thy WORD above all thy NAME."   **— Psalms 138:2**

➲ Let us set OUR hearts upon magnifying His word.

In his classic work on Baptist churches, Edward Hisox writes

"The Bible is a Divine Revelation given of God to men, and is a complete and infallible guide and standard of authority in all matters of religion and morals;

- Whatever it teaches is to be BELIEVED,

- And whatever it commands is to be OBEYED;

- Whatever it commends is to be ACCEPTED as both right and useful;

- Whatever it condemns is to be AVOIDED as both wrong and hurtful;

- But what it neither commands nor teaches is not to be imposed on the conscience as of religious obligation.

---

[8] **John Dryden** (1631-1700) "Poet Laureate" of England (1668-1689), so dominated the literary life of *Restoration England* that the period is known in literary circles as the *Age of Dryden*.

"The New Testament is

- The constitution of Christianity,

- The charter of the Christian Church,

- The only authoritative code of ecclesiastical law,

- And the warrant and justification of all Christian institutions.

- In it alone is life and immortality brought to light,

- The way of escape from wrath revealed,

- And all things necessary to salvation made plain;

- While its messages are a gospel of peace on earth and of hope to a lost world."[9]

We must be as the Thessalonians

"For this cause also thank we God without ceasing, because, when ye received the word of God which ye heard of us, ye received it not as the word of men, but as it is in truth, the word of God, which effectually worketh also in you that believe."

— I Thessalonians 2:13

We believe the Holy Bible is given to us by the God who created all things by His word. Therefore, it is the basis of all other authority, not only in spiritual matters, but in moral and legal matters as well.

"Judge Roy Moore points out that the '[L]aws of England as well as the Common Law upon which it was based presuppose a belief in God and His will, is the basis of all law.'"[10]

---

[9] **Edward T. Hiscox**, The New Directory for Baptist Churches, (1859) Chapter One, "Propositions and Statements", Propositions 1-2.

[10] **D. James Kennedy** and **Jerry Newcombe**, What If The Bible Had Never Been Written; (Thomas Nelson Publishers), Their quote from and unpublished "Affidavit and Statement of Facts" by Alabama Supreme Court Judge Roy Moore.

Judge Moore gave testimony in a court of law that "a belief in God and His will" is the basis of all human law and, even more, church government and life. Biblical authority is the first and foremost doctrine of the Baptist faith.

"Final authority" is the primary issue Christians must address today. Sadly, the worst attacks on the word of God are no longer from atheists and infidels, but from preachers and teachers within the Church itself. I am going to give some illustrations now, and show why we must know what we believe about the precious Book that is our light and life (John 6:63).

Mormons claim that the <u>Book of Mormon</u>, the <u>Pearl of Great Price</u> and the <u>Doctrines and Covenants</u> are all inspired by God and have equal or greater authority than the Holy Bible.

Roman Catholics also have another authority *above* the Holy Bible; the Catholic church itself, along with a long list of traditions and interpretations of the scripture by the church fathers and the Pope added.

To see just what the Roman Catholic church teaches concerning authority and inerrancy of scripture, I will quote from two articles found on the *Catholic Answers* [11] Internet web site.

"WHAT'S YOUR AUTHORITY?" [12]

"This is nothing fancy, just a little script you might learn from. In Catholic Answers' seminars we try to emphasize the point that you should always demand that a missionary who comes to your door first establish his AUTHORITY for what he is going to tell you, and only then proceed to discuss the particular issues he has in mind.

---

[11] *Catholic Answers* is one of the nation's largest lay-run apostolates of Catholic apologetics and evangelization. Directed by Karl Keating. (all caps, other than title, are mine for emphasis.)

[12] "What's Your Authority?" *Catholic Answers,* (6/7/2011) *NIHIL OBSTAT:* I have concluded that the materials presented in this work are free of doctrinal or moral errors. Bernadeane Carr, *STL, Censor Librorum,* August 10, 2004. *IMPRIMATUR:* In accord with 1983 CIC 827 permission to publish this work is hereby granted. Robert H. Brom, Bishop of San Diego, August 10, 2004. www.catholic.com/library/What_Your_Authority.asp

"By 'AUTHORITY,' we don't mean his personal or academic credentials. We mean his AUTHORITY to claim he can rightly interpret the Bible. The missionary (unless he is a Mormon, of course, in which case his AUTHORITY is the Book of Mormon) will always claim to fall back on the AUTHORITY of Scripture. 'Scripture says this' or 'Scripture proves that,' he will tell you.

"So before you turn to the verses he brings up, and thus to the topic he brings up, demand that he demonstrate a few things.

> "<u>FIRST</u>,   ask him to prove from the Bible that the Bible is the only rule of faith (if he's an Evangelical or Fundamentalist Protestant he holds to the Reformation theory of *sola scriptura*— THE BIBLE ALONE).

> "<u>SECOND</u>,   have him tell you how he knows which books belong in the Bible in the first place.

> "<u>THIRD</u>,   require that he prove to you both that he has the AUTHORITY to interpret the Bible for you (remember that his doctrines will almost always be drawn from *interpretations* of the sacred text RATHER THAN THE WORDS THEMSELVES) and that his interpretations will always be accurate."

"SCRIPTURE AND TRADITION [13]

"Protestants claim the Bible is the only rule of faith, meaning that it contains all of the material one needs for theology and that this material is sufficiently clear that one does not need apostolic tradition or the Church's magisterium (teaching AUTHORITY) to help one understand it. In the Protestant view, the whole of Christian truth is found within the Bible's pages. Anything extraneous to the Bible is simply non-authoritative, unnecessary, or wrong— and may well hinder one in coming to God.

---

[13] "Scripture and Tradition," *Catholic Answers*
www.catholic.com/library/What_Your_Authority.asp,6/7/2011

"Catholics, on the other hand, recognize that the Bible does not endorse this view and that, in fact, it is repudiated in Scripture. The true 'rule of faith'— as expressed in the Bible itself— is Scripture PLUS apostolic tradition, as manifested in the living teaching AUTHORITY of the Catholic Church, to which were entrusted the oral teachings of Jesus and the apostles, along with the AUTHORITY to interpret Scripture correctly.

"In the Second Vatican Council's document on divine revelation, *Dei Verbum* (Latin: 'The Word of God'), the relationship between Tradition and Scripture is explained:

> 'Hence there exists a close connection and communication between sacred Tradition and sacred Scripture. For both of them, flowing from the same divine wellspring, in a certain way merge into a unity and tend toward the same end. For sacred Scripture is the word of God inasmuch as it is consigned to writing under the inspiration of the divine Spirit. To the successors of the apostles, sacred Tradition hands on in its full purity God's word, which was entrusted to the apostles by Christ the Lord and the Holy Spirit.'

> 'Thus, by the light of the Spirit of truth, these successors can in their preaching preserve this word of God faithfully, explain it, and make it more widely known. Consequently it is not from sacred Scripture alone that the Church draws her certainty about everything which has been revealed. Therefore both sacred Tradition and sacred Scripture are to be accepted and venerated with the same devotion and reverence.'

"The Indefectible Church [14]

"The task is to determine what constitutes authentic tradition. How can we know which traditions are apostolic and which are merely human? The answer is the same as how we know which scriptures are apostolic and which are merely human— by listening to the magisterium or teaching AUTHORITY of Christ's Church. Without the Catholic Church's teaching AUTHORITY, we would not know with

---

[14] **Indefectible** 1. Having the ability to resist decay or failure; lasting. 2. Having no flaw or defect; perfect. American Heritage Dictionary

certainty which purported books of Scripture are authentic. If the Church revealed to us the canon of Scripture, it can also reveal to us the 'canon of Tradition' by establishing which traditions have been passed down from the apostles. After all, Christ promised that the gates of hell would not prevail against the Church (Matthew 16:18) and the New Testament itself declares the Church to be 'the pillar and foundation of the truth' (I Timothy 3:15)."

We can see from these two articles just how important "the words themselves" are to the believer. The Roman Catholic church claims to be "indefectible" (perfect), and therefore it alone has the authority to interpret scripture (even above comparing scripture with scripture). As Bible-believing Baptists our primary interest lies in **what "the words themselves" SAY**, and not someone's private "interpretation." So, **what *does* the Bible SAY?** I put this question before you now, "Could you open your Bible right now and give scripture to answer the questions that were posed, and the charges that were made by *Catholic Answers* in the above excerpt from their website?" You may never be confronted with these questions, but for your own peace of mind, you should be prepared to answer them. Furthermore, if you have never had to show anyone what you believe, from the Bible, then it is obvious that you are not witnessing to others. The one who is actively presenting the gospel will be confronted with all kinds of questions and challenges that you must be ready to respond to biblically (I Peter 3:15).

"Catholic Answers" urges their readers to require the Bible-believing soulwinner to establish, from the Bible, why he believes his Bible to be the final authority for what he believes and teaches. You know, that is a reasonable request, and one that is an excellent starting place. This should easily work to the advantage of the Christian who knows what the Bible **SAYS**.

We will only need a King James Bible for this entire exercise, because we believe what it SAYS. Unlike some, we need not carry around a Hebrew Old Testament, Greek New Testament, a Hebrew and a Greek lexicon, the writings of the church fathers, and several sets of commentaries to find what "THE WORDS THEMSELVES" really are.

➲ **First of all**, we should be able to prove, *from our Bible,*[15] that it alone, is the final AUTHORITY for what we believe.

In other words, we do not have to consult with an official representative of a religious group, or some ancient writings of highly esteemed men, or learn a foreign language in order to establish and teach the doctrines we believe and live by. That is why we are called Bible believers. We believe what the Bible in our hand and in our own tongue SAYS. We believe the Bible is our final authority because:

1. The Bible is the written record of God's words.

> "If we receive the witness of men, <u>the witness of God is greater</u>: for this is the witness of God which he hath testified of his Son.
>
> "He that believeth on the Son of God hath the witness in himself: he that believeth not God hath made him a liar; because he believeth not <u>the record</u> that God gave of his Son.
>
> "And <u>this is the record</u>, that God hath given to us eternal life, and this life is in his Son.
>
> "He that hath the Son hath life; and he that hath not the Son of God hath not life.
>
> "<u>These things have I written</u> unto you that believe on the name of the Son of God; <u>that ye may know</u> that ye have eternal life, and that ye may believe on the name of the Son of God."
>
> **— I John 5:9-13**

---

[15] When I refer to the "Bible," I mean only a King James 1611 authorized version of the Bible we can hold in our hands.

2. His words are all that are necessary for us to live by.

"Jesus answered and said unto him, If a man love me, he will keep <u>my WORDS</u>: and my Father will love him, and we will come unto him, and make our abode with him." — John 14:23

"Heaven and earth shall pass away, but <u>my WORDS</u> shall not pass away." — Matthew 24:35

"He that rejecteth me, and receiveth not <u>my WORDS</u>, hath one that judgeth him: <u>the word that I have spoken</u>, the same shall judge him in the last day." — John 12:48

"Let thy mercies come also unto me, O LORD, even thy salvation, according to <u>thy word</u>.

"So shall I have wherewith to answer him that reproacheth me: for I trust in <u>thy word</u>."

— Psalms 119:41-42

"For he mightily convinced the Jews, and that publickly, shewing by <u>the scriptures</u> that Jesus was Christ." — Acts 18:28

"The Revelation of Jesus Christ, <u>which God gave unto him</u>, to shew unto his servants things which must shortly come to pass; and he sent and signified it by his angel unto his servant John:

"Who bare RECORD of <u>the word of God</u>, and of <u>the testimony of Jesus Christ</u>, and of all things that he saw."

— Revelation 1:1-2

3. The Bible is the word of God.

"For this cause also thank we God without ceasing, because, when ye received <u>the word of God</u> which ye heard of us, ye received it not as the word of men, but as it is in truth, <u>the word of God</u>, which effectually worketh also in you that believe."

— I Thessalonians 2:13

4. The Bible is inspired by God.

"And that from a child thou hast known the <u>holy scriptures,</u> which are able to make thee wise unto salvation through faith which is in Christ Jesus.

"All <u>scripture is given by inspiration of God,</u> and is profitable for doctrine, for reproof, for correction, for instruction in righteousness:

"That the man of God may be perfect, throughly[16] furnished unto all good works."

　　　　　　　　　　　　　— II Timothy 3:15-17[17]

5. The Bible is established forever.

"Quicken me after thy lovingkindness; so shall I keep the <u>testimony of thy mouth.</u>

"For ever, O LORD, <u>thy word</u> is settled in heaven."

　　　　　　　　　　　　　— Psalms 119:88-89

6. The Bible is exalted above all things.

"I will worship toward thy holy temple, and praise thy name for thy lovingkindness and for thy truth: for thou hast magnified <u>thy word</u> above all thy name."

　　　　　　　　　　　　　— Psalms 138:2

7. His words are pure and can keep us pure.

"<u>The words of the LORD are pure words</u>: as silver tried in a furnace of earth, purified seven times."

　　　　　　　　　　　　　— Psalms 12:6

"Wherewithal shall a young man cleanse his way? by taking heed thereto according to <u>thy word.</u>"

"With my whole heart have I sought thee: O let me not wander from <u>thy commandments.</u>

---

[16] **Thorough** 1. Exhaustively complete: a thorough search. 2. Painstakingly accurate or careful: thorough research. 3. Absolute; utter: a thorough pleasure. ("Throughly" is the old spelling, "thoroughly" is today's spelling. <u>American Heritage Dictionary</u>

[17] While this verse can be used to establish that all scripture is "inspired," we have seen that the Catholic is told it is not "sufficient" (all that is needed). But, it is sufficient for us.

"<u>Thy word</u> have I hid in mine heart, that I might not sin against thee."

— Psalms 119:9-11

8. His words are Spirit and life.

"Verily, verily, I say unto you, He that heareth <u>my word</u>, and believeth on him that sent me, hath everlasting life, and shall not come into condemnation; but is passed from death unto <u>life</u>."   — John 5:24

"It is the spirit that quickeneth; the flesh profiteth nothing: <u>the words that I speak unto you, they are spirit, and they are life</u>."   — John 6:63

"Holding forth <u>the word of life</u>; that I may rejoice in the day of Christ, that I have not run in vain, neither laboured in vain."   — Philippians 2:16

9. God has promised to preserve His words.[18]

"Thou shalt keep them, O LORD, thou shalt preserve them from this generation for ever."

— Psalms 12:7

From the Bible, we understand that God Himself, and not man, has preserved God's very words.

<u>Our Savior proclaimed</u>

"It is written, Man shall not live by bread alone, but by EVERY WORD that proceedeth out of the mouth of God."   — Matthew 4:4

If we do not have "every word," how then shall we live; on the mere crust and crumbs of man's traditions and interpretations?

---

[18] **God has preserved His words** *in spite of man*, **not with the help of man.** Some claim the King James Bible is superior to other translations, because of the superior scholarship of its translators. However, although God did use those learned men, we do not trust the scholarship of the saved, to preserve the word of God, any more than we trust the scholarship of the unsaved. We believe that "**Our help cometh from the Lord**" (Psalm 121:2).

Where are these very words by which man is to live? We believe we have them faithfully preserved in our King James Bible.

Why would we not expect that He would preserve them, for it is by His words that man will be judged in the last day.

> "**The word that I have spoken, the same shall judge him in the last day.**"   **— John 12:48**

10. The Bible is Truth.

> "**Sanctify them through thy truth: thy word is truth.**"
>   **— John 17:17**

> "**Thy word is true from the beginning: and every one of thy righteous judgments endureth for ever.**"
>   **— Psalms 119:160**

11. The Bible is the power of God.

> "**Jesus answered and said unto them, Ye do err, not knowing the scriptures, nor the power of God.**"
>   **— Matthew 22:29**

12. The Bible is the gospel of salvation.

> "**For I am not ashamed of the gospel of Christ: for it is the power of God unto salvation to every one that believeth; to the Jew first, and also to the Greek.**
>
> "**For therein is the righteousness of God revealed from faith to faith: as it is written, The just shall live by faith.**"
>   **— Romans 1:16-17**

> "**In whom ye also trusted, after that ye heard the word of truth, the gospel of your salvation: in whom also after that ye believed, ye were sealed with that holy Spirit of promise,**"   **— Ephesians 1:13**

13. His word is incorruptible and eternal.

> "**Being born again, not of corruptible seed, but of incorruptible, by the word of God, which liveth and abideth for ever.**"   **— I Peter 1:23**

14. The Bible is the sword of the Spirit.

"And take the helmet of salvation, and the sword of the Spirit, which is <u>the word of God</u>:"

— Ephesians 6:17

15. The Bible imparts faith to the hearer.

"For whosoever shall call upon the name of the Lord shall be saved.

"How then shall they call on him in whom they have not believed? and how shall they believe in him of whom they have not heard? and how shall they hear without a preacher?

"And how shall they preach, except they be sent? as it is written, How beautiful are the feet of them that preach the gospel of peace, and bring glad tidings of good things!

"But they have not all obeyed the gospel. For Esaias saith, Lord, who hath believed our report?

"So then faith cometh by hearing, and hearing by <u>the word of God</u>."

— Romans 10:13-17

16. The Bible is alive, piercing and discerning.

"For <u>the word of God</u> is quick, and powerful, and sharper than any twoedged sword, piercing even to the dividing asunder of soul and spirit, and of the joints and marrow, and is a discerner of the thoughts and intents of the heart.

"Neither is there any creature that is not manifest in <u>his</u> sight: but all things are naked and opened unto the eyes of <u>him</u> with whom we have to do."

— Hebrews 4:12-13

17. The word of truth begets us spiritually.

"Of his own will begat he us with <u>the word of truth</u>, that we should be a kind of firstfruits of his creatures."   — James 1:18

18. The word of God births us spiritually.

"Being born again, not of corruptible seed, but of incorruptible, by the word of God, which liveth and abideth for ever." — I Peter 1:23

19. The Bible lights our path.

"Thy word is a lamp unto my feet, and a light unto my path." — Psalms 119:105

20. His word is righteousness.

"My tongue shall speak of thy word: for all thy commandments are righteousness." — Psalms 119:172

Certainly this list does not exhaust the attributes and work of the word of God. However, it should be sufficient to demonstrate that if the Bible is truly God's word, then it is without controversy the highest and purest authority in the universe. There is nothing in heaven or earth to compare with it, and why should we accept any frail carnal authority as equal to or above it?

➲ **Secondly,** we should be able to show why we accept only the books in our King James English Bible as scripture.[19]

"What determined which books belong in the Bible? How did we end up with 39 books in the Old Testament and 27 books in the New Testament? These questions are answered in a discussion of the 'canon of Scripture.' The word 'canon' means 'a measuring device' or 'a standard.'

"Out of the many religious writings that have been circulated, only 66 books were accepted as inspired by God. While some were recognized immediately as authentic, it took some time for others to be endorsed as Scripture. Throughout the process, however, the canon of Scripture was being determined by God, not by man."[20]

---

[19] The **Apocrypha** is not part of SCRIPTURE. In fact the word Apocrypha means "Writings or statements of questionable authorship or authenticity." American Heritage Dictionary

[20] **Richard DeHaan**, Can I Really Trust the Bible? (Radio Bible Class)

For some, this is a complex issue involving the examination of ancient manuscripts, Greek and Hebrew texts and scholarship of men. But, the Bible-believer takes it by faith that God, who gave the scriptures, is able to preserve them (Psalm 68:11; 12:6,7). Still, there is plenty of manuscript evidence to support our beliefs, if one is so inclined to search it out.

   1. Jesus accepted the Jewish Old Testament canon.[21]

> **"And he said unto them, These are <u>the words which I spake</u> unto you, while I was yet with you, that all things must be fulfilled, <u>which were written</u> in THE LAW of Moses, and in THE PROPHETS, and in THE PSALMS, concerning me.**

> **"Then opened he their understanding, that they might understand <u>the scriptures,</u>**

> **"And said unto them, Thus <u>it is written</u>, and thus it behoved Christ to suffer, and to rise from the dead the third day:**

> **"And that repentance and remission of sins should be preached in his name among all nations, beginning at Jerusalem."**

> **— Luke 24:44-47** [22,23]

---

[21] This means that the *Council of Trent* in 1500 "anathematized' the Lord Jesus Christ when they said "anyone who doesn't accept the apocrypha as part of the Old Testament is accursed."

[22] Albert Barnes Notes on the New Testament, 'In **the law of Moses.'** The five books of Moses— Genesis, Exodus, Leviticus, Numbers, Deuteronomy. Among the Jews this was the first division of the Old Testament, and was called the law.

'**The prophets.'** This was the second and largest part of the Hebrew Scriptures. It comprehended the books of Joshua, Judges, 1st and 2nd Samuel, 1st and 2nd Kings, which were called the former prophets; and Isaiah, Jeremiah, Ezekiel, and the twelve smaller books from Daniel to Malachi, which were called the latter prophets.

'**The psalms.'** The word here used probably means what were comprehended under the name of 'Hagiographa,' or holy writings. This consisted of the Psalms, Proverbs, Job, Song of Solomon, Ruth, Lamentations, Ecclesiastes, Esther, Daniel, Ezra, and Nehemiah, and the two books of Chronicles. This division of the Old Testament was in use long before the time of Christ…"

[23] **Peter S. Ruckman,** Ruckman's Bible References, [This passage is] "crucial, for it shows that Christ accepted the basic, traditional Old Testament canon recognized by all *orthodox Jews,* before His time and after His time; that is, *He did not accept*

> "That upon you may come all the righteous blood shed upon the earth, <u>from the blood of righteous Abel unto the blood of Zacharias</u> son of Barachias, whom ye slew between the temple and the altar."
>
> — Matthew 23:35 [24]

2. The New Testament books were clearly established.

The authors of the New Testament books were all Jews and they were all apostles. The only exceptions were Mark and Luke, but they were mentioned by the apostles as having been their associates in the ministry. Furthermore, they were all "eyewitnesses" of the events they wrote about. Finally, there was Paul, the apostle to the Gentiles, to whom the "gospel of the grace of God" was revealed. The New Testament scripture was not chosen from a vast number of writings of questionable authenticity. Those commonly accepted by the churches as being authentic were chosen, while other *spurious* writings were rejected.

<u>The apostles were eyewitnesses</u>

> "And as they thus spake, <u>Jesus himself stood in the midst of them</u>, and saith unto them, Peace be unto you.
>
> "But they were terrified and affrighted, and supposed that they had seen a spirit.
>
> "And he said unto them, Why are ye troubled? and why do thoughts arise in your hearts?
>
> "Behold my hands and my feet, that it is I myself: handle me, and see; for a spirit hath not flesh and bones, as ye see me have.
>
> "And when he had thus spoken, he shewed them his hands and his feet.

---

the Scriptural canon defined by the Roman Catholic Church at the Council of Trent. This was unfortunate for Him, because the Vatican put a curse on *any* man who did NOT accept their canon as correct. *Rome is the only professing "Christian" organization to officially curse Jesus Christ."*

[24] The arrangement of the books in Jewish canon puts Genesis first and the two books of Chronicles last. So, Christ has established the canon of scripture and it excluded the Apocrypha. Abel is slain in Genesis; Zacharias, is Zechariah, whose death is recorded in II Chronicles 24:20-21.

"And while they yet believed not for joy, and wondered, he said unto them, Have ye here any meat?

"And they gave him a piece of a broiled fish, and of an honeycomb. And he took it, and did eat before them.

"And he said unto them, <u>These are the words which I spake unto you</u>, while I was yet with you, that all things must be fulfilled, which were written in the law of Moses, and in the prophets, and in the psalms, concerning me.

"<u>Then opened he their understanding, that they might understand the scriptures</u>,

"<u>And said unto them</u>, Thus it is written, and thus it behoved Christ to suffer, and to rise from the dead the third day:

"And that repentance and remission of sins should be preached in his name among all nations, beginning at Jerusalem.

'AND <u>YE ARE WITNESSES</u> OF THESE THINGS.'

— Luke 24:36-48

"Moreover, brethren, I declare unto you the gospel which I preached unto you, which also ye have received, and wherein ye stand;

"By which also ye are saved, if ye keep in memory what I preached unto you, unless ye have believed in vain.

"For I delivered unto you first of all that which I also received, how that Christ died for our sins according to the scriptures;

"And that he was buried, and that he rose again the third day according to the scriptures:

"<u>And that he was seen of Cephas, then of the twelve:</u>

"After that, he was seen of above five hundred brethren at once; of whom the greater part remain unto this present, but some are fallen asleep.

"After that, he was seen of James; then of all the apostles.

"And last of all he was seen of me also, as of one born out of due time."
— I Corinthians 15:1-8

Richard DeHaan says

"The acceptance of the New Testament books was based on the test of apostleship. They were received if they were written by an apostle, such as Peter or John, or by someone close to an apostle, such as Luke or Mark, who had apostolic authorization. We know that some false accounts of Christ's life were being distributed (Luke 1:1-4), as well as some false epistles (II Thessalonians 2:2). Therefore, positive identification of the New Testament books was necessary.

"The church fathers supported the inspiration of the New Testament canon and carefully identified and eliminated questionable works. The Councils of Hippo (AUTHORITY 393) and Carthage (AD 397) accepted the 27 books that now appear in the New Testament." [25]

As J.I. Packer said

"The church no more gave us the New Testament canon than Sir Isaac Newton gave us the force of gravity. God gave us gravity by His work of creation, and similarly He gave us the New Testament canon by inspiring the original books that make it up." [26]

Dr. H.L. Wilmington says

"During the Third Council of Carthage, held in AD 397, the twenty-seven New Testament books were declared to be canonical. However, it absolutely must be understood that the Bible is not *an authorized collection of books,* but rather *a collection of authorized books.* In other words, the twenty-seven New Testament books were not inspired because the Carthage Council proclaimed them to be, but

---

[25] **Richard DeHaan,** Can I Really Trust the Bible? (Radio Bible Class)

[26] **J.I. Packer,** God Speaks to Man

rather the Council proclaimed them to be such because they were already inspired."[27]

When the "church fathers" walked into their meeting room with all their knowledge and manuscripts, God, in eternity, already had the finished copy of the book they would produce. He did not receive it from them, they received it from Him. The canon of scripture was not accepted by God because these men said so; they accepted those books because God ordained it. The canon of scripture was not settled by the Council of Carthage— it was settled in eternity by the Lord Himself, then revealed to man.

We read in the scripture:

"For ever, O LORD, thy word is settled in heaven."

— Psalms 119:89

While we emphasize the providence of God in the preservation of scripture, others emphasize man's scholarship as the key to its preservation and accuracy. Some seem to have more faith in man than they have in God.

It is not in vain that we are instructed by scripture:

"It is better to trust in the LORD than to put confidence in man."   — Psalms 118:8

3. The witness of history confirms the veracity of scripture.

Today, it is much easier to see that the sixty-six books that comprise the Old and New Testaments of our Bible are indeed inspired scripture. The passing of time has afforded us certain proofs that demonstrate the integrity of our divinely inspired and preserved Bible.

a. Internal Evidence

The layout of the chapters and verses of the book of Isaiah in the King James English Bible is amazing.

---

[27] **H.L. Willmington**, Willmington's Guide to the Bible Tyndale House Publishers

There are SIXTY-SIX books in our King James Bible and there are SIXTY-SIX chapters in the book of Isaiah.

And, just as there are two parts to the Bible— the Old Testament and the New Testament, there are two parts to the book of Isaiah. You may think, "Well, that is interesting, but why is it so significant." (KEEP READING.) In the FORTIETH chapter of Isaiah, there is such an obvious **change** in the style of writing that the liberals say it must have been written by a different author.[28] The last chapter before the break is Isaiah chapter THIRTY-NINE. (There are THIRTY-NINE books in the Old Testament.)

It is no coincidence that the prophecies found in chapter FORTY of Isaiah are fulfilled in the FORTIETH book of the Bible. Therefore, we find that the THIRD verse of Isaiah chapter FORTY, is just like the THIRD verse in the THIRD chapter of Matthew of the New Testament. In this FORTIETH chapter, we see Isaiah's prophecy of the coming Kingdom of Heaven. John the Baptist shows up in the FORTIETH book of the Bible preaching *"[R]epent ye: for the kingdom of heaven is at hand"* and, quoting Isaiah, *"Prepare ye the way of the LORD."*

But, that is not all. Even more interesting is the fact that the SIXTY-SIXTH chapter of Isaiah (i.e. verses 8, 15, 16, 21-24) deals with the second advent and the Millennium, just like Revelation does (which just happens to be the SIXTY-SIXTH book of the Bible).

Beloved, there is no book in the universe like the Bible. Even the arrangement of the books, the chapters and the verses seem to be according to God's design.

So, we are not surprised that the FIRST chapter of Isaiah (cf. Isaiah 1:2, "Hear, O heavens, and give ear, O earth: for the LORD hath spoken") is like the FIRST book of the Bible (Genesis chapter one) where God SPOKE, and the heavens and Earth were created.

---

[28] The change in style, about which so much has been said, is no more remarkable than the change of theme. A prophet who was also a patriot would not write of the sins and coming captivity of his people in the same exultant and joyous style which he would use to describe their redemption, blessing and power. In John 12:37-44 quotations from Isaiah chapter 53 and Isaiah chapter 6 are both ascribed to Isaiah. (the note for Isaiah 40:1). The Scofield Reference Bible

What is even more amazing is that Isaiah had no idea that there would be thirty-nine books in the completed Old Testament, nor that there would be twenty-seven books of New Testament writings, making a total of sixty-six in the whole Bible. But, somebody knew it, and arranged the book of Isaiah so as to show it beforehand. Now, you couldn't discover this from the Hebrew, because the order of the books is different in the Hebrew. Neither could you find it in a Catholic Bible, because it has added the Apocrypha as part of scripture. As Dr. Peter Ruckman would say, "Ah, the wonders of the 'original English.'"

b. Harmony of Doctrine

By rightly dividing the word, we find there are no contradictions nor errors in the holy scriptures. This is not true of the extraneous books rejected as scripture.

Problems in understanding the word of God come from trying to make scripture conform to a preconceived theology. A further source of difficulty comes from trying to understand God's word with man's limited human faculties apart from the Spirit of God.

> **"Be ye not as the horse, or as the mule, which have no understanding: whose mouth must be held in with bit and bridle, lest they come near unto thee."** — Psalms 32:9

> **"Trust in the LORD with all thine heart; and lean not unto thine own understanding."** — Proverbs 3:5

> **"Desiring to be teachers of the law; understanding neither what they say, nor whereof they affirm."** — I Timothy 1:7

If there is something outside the sixty-six books of our Holy Bible that is different from what it teaches, then we do not accept it. If there is anything that teaches the same thing, then we do not need it. We are confident that what we have is sufficient.

Three times scripture commands us NOT TO ADD to the word of God— **once,** at the beginning, **again,** in the middle and then **finally,** at the end.

> "Ye <u>shall not add</u> unto the word which I command you, <u>neither shall ye diminish</u> ought from it, that ye may keep the commandments of the LORD your God which **I command you."** — **Deuteronomy 4:2**

> "<u>Add thou not</u> unto his words, lest he reprove thee, and thou be found a liar." — **Proverbs 30:6**

> "For I testify unto every man that heareth the words of the prophecy of this book, <u>If any man shall add unto these things, God shall add unto him the plagues that are written in this book</u>:"
> — **Revelation 22:18**

⊃ And **thirdly,** we should be able to prove *from scripture* why we believe <u>the AUTHORITY of the Bible is all we need</u> to "interpret the Bible" (understand what it SAYS) and that our interpretations will always be accurate.

As we have already seen from what is being taught by the *Catholic Answers* ministry, they believe that our "...doctrines will almost always be drawn from *interpretations* of the sacred text rather than THE WORDS THEMSELVES."

While it is obvious that many verses require *some* interpretation, we aim to show that the Bible interprets itself. And, **we, Bible-believers, confess to emphasizing "THE WORDS THEMSELVES."** In plainer words, we believe the Bible means what it says, and says what it means.

The Lord Jesus Christ did not spend His time with scholars, but with twelve common, hard working, uneducated men. Why then would it take a scholar to understand the scriptures that He committed to them.

The Bible is like an ocean; there are parts where even a baby wade in, but plenty enough for a scholar to drown in.

Don't get me wrong, there is nothing wrong with education; as long as it is subject to the word of God and not contrariwise. Furthermore, we are challenged by "Catholic Answers" ministry to show that "our interpretations will always be accurate."

1. **REMEMBER:** The only way to understand the Bible is by rightly dividing the word by Dispensational Theology

A faulty systematic theology will produce many apparent contradictions in scripture. Since the Catholic theologian's theology is wrong, he knows he cannot explain much of the Bible; therefore, he thinks no one else can either. While no one claims to understand *every* verse of scripture perfectly, anyone using dispensational theology *can* understand the correct doctrinal application for salvation and living a godly life. Also, when we rightly divide the word of truth, we can understand what a verse does not mean, even if we do not know what it does mean. Furthermore, we can see plainly whether it applies to the believer in the church age.

No man, least of all a Roman Catholic priest, can guarantee *every* interpretation of *every* verse of scripture will be one-hundred percent accurate. There are still some verses I do not really understand. Let's just face it, our frail, limited flesh is not capable of understanding everything now. Like Mark Twain said many years ago, *"I am not worried about the things in the Bible I don't understand; I am worried about the things I do understand."* There is plenty that we believers *do understand* about the Bible, and we certainly are *not doing* all we know. Until we obey what we already know, we need not be overly concerned about what we do not know.

Even as the apostle Paul wrote

"For we know in part, and we prophesy in part.

"But when that which is perfect is come, then that which is in part shall be done away.

> "When I was a child, I spake as a child, I under-
> stood as a child, I thought as a child: but when I
> became a man, I put away childish things.
>
> "For now we see through a glass, darkly; but then
> face to face: now I know in part; but then shall I know
> even as also I am known."
> — I Corinthians 13:9-12

2. REMEMBER: The word of God is correctly interpreted by the Literal Grammatical-Historical Method

Literal — We are to take the words of the Bible to mean what they say in the plain sense in which they are recorded. It has been well said, "If the literal sense makes good sense, seek no other sense, lest it result in nonsense." Unless the passage is *obviously* figurative, it is always to be taken in the plain and common sense.

Grammatical — We are to follow the normal grammatical rules of literature, including grammatical tools like similes, metaphors, etc. May I add, that most pastors do not have nearly as good a grasp of the English language as they think they do. Before studying Greek and Hebrew we ought to become well learned in the English language. Thereby, understanding of many passages would be enhanced and so-called problems resolved. "Whatsoever thy hand findeth to do, do it with thy might..." (Ecclesiastes 9:10) applies to the preacher and student of the word of God.

Historical — We are to look at a passage of scripture in the light of the customs and culture of its day and historical context. Today, there are many good Bible handbooks and commentaries to aid us in the process of understanding the people and places of the Bible.

Pastor Cooper Abrams says it well

"Everything depends on the method of interpretation.

"I Corinthians 14:33, says 'God is not the author of confusion.' Apparently, there has been great latitude taken in the

interpretation of what the Bible says. The word 'interpretation' means to arrive at the original meaning the writer
intended when he penned the words. The original meaning
the author intended is the interpretation and must be found
before you can apply it or make application of the passage.
A faulty interpretation will produce a faulty application and
therefore it is vital to correctly interpret the Scriptures.

"The great need today... in determining what the Bible
really teaches, is a correct method of interpretation. If the
Bible is the Word of God and God's revelation to man, then
surely God would not give us His revelation without a way
to discern what He meant. For God NOT to give us a way
to interpret the Bible is to leave the interpretation of Scripture to human wisdom that is at best faulty. To have the
interpretation of Scripture rest on man's wisdom is to have
'flesh' interpreting that which is spiritual...

"The problem today, is NOT, that God did not give us a
method of interpretation. God did give us a method! But,
man has either refused to use it, or has not been diligent in
seeking it! The method that God gave is the LITERAL
METHOD, or what man has labeled the Grammatical-
Historical method. The Grammatical-Historical method
interprets Scripture by taking into consideration the context
of a passage, the grammatical usage of the words and the
historical setting in which they were written. The literal
method, 'lets Scripture interpret Scripture'...

"When God inspired the writers to use a word, it was
because that word conveyed a certain meaning. It communicated a certain meaning to those who read it. This means
that if we find what was the correct meaning of the word,
considering its context, normal and customary usage at the
time it was used, we can know the correct interpretation." [29]

Hank Hanegraaff says

"Principles of biblical interpretation ought to be determined before developing one's theology, but in practice the
reverse is often true. Cultists in particular consistently read
their deviant theologies into the biblical text instead of
allowing the text to speak for itself. 'Faith' teachers

---

[29] **Cooper P. Abrams III**, "Biblical Principles for Interpreting the God's Word"
www.bible-truth.org/Principles.htm

(so-called) are also guilty of this practice, as I document in my book Christianity in Crisis.

"In view of this growing problem, it would be productive to consider some of the primary principles of hermeneutics. Before you run off because of the formidable sound of this term, however, let me quickly point out that hermeneutics is simply a 'fifty-cent' word that describes the science of biblical interpretation. The purpose of hermeneutics is to provide the student of Scripture with basic guidelines and rules for "rightly dividing the word of truth" (II Timothy 2:15)...

"Literal Interpretation

"In simple terms, this means that we are to interpret the Word of God just as we interpret other forms of communication— in its most obvious and literal sense. Most often, the biblical authors employed literal statements to communicate their ideas (such as when the apostle Paul said of Jesus, 'By Him all things were created, both in the heavens and on earth'— Colossians 1:16). And where the biblical writers express their ideas in literal statements, the interpreter must take those statements in a literal sense. In this way, the interpreter will grasp the intended meaning of the writer.

"Of course, this is not to deny that Scripture employs figures of speech. Indeed, the biblical writers often used figurative language to communicate truth in a graphic way. And, in most cases, the meaning of such language is clear from the context. When Jesus says He is 'the door' (John 10:7), for example, it is obvious He is not saying He is composed of wood and hinges. Rather, He is the 'way' to salvation."[30]

German theologian, Eugene Klug adds

"Clearly, if the Bible does not mean what it *appears* to mean and does not teach what is *seems* to teach, the door opens wide for an infinite number of new interpretations, teachings, and styles of church life.[31]

---

[30] **Hank Hanegraaff**, "L-I-G-H-T-S to the Word of God," (the Bible Answer Man) www.oneplace.com/Ministries/Bible_Answer_Man/Article.asp?article_id=82

[31] **Eugene F.A. Klug**, *Evangelium* "'Sensus Literalis' das Wort in den Wörtern, eine hermeneutische Meditation vom Verstehen der Bibel," 165-75, (December, 1985)

'It is a fundamental principle to assume that there is one intended, literal, proper sense to any given passage in Scripture ('sensus literalis unus est'); also that the Scripture is its own best interpreter ('Scriptura Scripturam interpretat' or 'Scriptura sui ipsius interpres')... The literal sense thus always stands first and each interpreter must guard against cluttering that which is being communicated with his own ideas, lest the meaning be lost.'"[32]

As we have read, "Catholic Answers" would *"require that (we) prove ...that (we have) the AUTHORITY to interpret the Bible..."* First of all, I might mention that no Catholic Pope or priest in the world has ever *proven* that the *Roman Catholic church* has any such authority. They simply bestow such authority upon themselves and expect us to follow them. However, *every* believer has the same *authority* to "rightly interpret" scripture for himself, just as those noble men of Berea that Luke spoke of in the book of Acts.

"And the brethren immediately sent away Paul and Silas by night unto Berea: who coming thither went into the synagogue of the Jews.

"These were more noble than those in Thessalonica, in that they received the word with all readiness of mind, and SEARCHED THE SCRIPTURES daily, whether those things were so."

— Acts 17:10-11

We are to learn what the Bible teaches, primarily by studying the Bible itself. That does not mean we are not to have teachers, but that even the teacher can be judged by the Bible he teaches.

Christ Himself admonished the Jews to:

"SEARCH THE SCRIPTURES; for in them ye think ye have eternal life: and THEY are they which TESTIFY OF ME."   **— John 5:39**

The prophet Isaiah proclaimed

"Seek ye out of the book of the LORD, and READ:..."
— Isaiah 34:16

---

[32] **John Montgomery**, "Legal Hermeneutics and the Interpretation of Scripture"

The Roman Catholic Church believes that it alone is the TRUE church, because of their interpretation of scripture. However, they also claim that the only way we can know what is scripture, is by the authority of the church. That is called "circular reasoning."

Furthermore, the Catholic church believes that scripture and tradition are equal when the Catholic church says so. But, that is "adding to" the word of God, which is forbidden by scripture. [33]

Below are some basic rules for studying the Bible that will help the student of the word of God to understand what he reads. [34]

"I. Never *Add To* Or *Take Away From* The Text Of The King James Bible

"Never study under a man who is a Bible corrector. When dealing with the Holy Bible, we will let the scriptures correct us, not contrariwise. Even while the Apostle Paul was still alive, men had already begun to correct the word of God.

"Paul sets himself apart from such, saying;

'For we are not as many, which corrupt the word of God...'   — II Corinthians 2:17

"Dr. Peter S. Ruckman says

'A Bible believer adjusts his theology to meet the demands of the TEXT— NOT adjust the TEXT to meet the demands of his theology.'

"II. Never Take A Verse Of Scripture Out Of Context

"It has been well said, *'A text without a context, is a pretext.'* Always study the verse in the light of its own setting. In other words, the portion of scripture we are studying (the text), taken without the setting of the verses surrounding it (context), is nothing more than a manner of promoting one's view without scriptural backing (pretext).

---

[33] See previous quotes from *Catholic Answers* and excerpt from the Catechism of the Catholic Church, in the Appendix at the end of this book.

[34] **Linton M. Smith**, The New Christian Series Bible course at www.valiantfortruth.net

" III. Never Attempt To Interpret A Verse Of Scripture You Understand, In The Light Of One You Do Not Understand

"Scripture should not be made to conform to a preconceived theology; on the contrary, scripture *determines* theology. As the light in the candlestick gave *'light over against it'* (Exodus 25:37), so scripture illuminates and explains scripture. The Bible is the *only* commentary that is *absolutely* dependable.

" IV. Never Go To *Scholarship* For The Definition Of Something The Bible Has Already Defined

"For example, the Bible definition of the words *'swine'* and *'dogs'* is found in Matthew 7:6 and II Peter 2:22.

"V. Always Ask *Who* Is Speaking And *To Whom*

" VI. Study to Understand the Customs, Culture and Historical Context Of The Passage at Hand

" VII. Always Take The Plain, Literal Meaning Of Every Verse Of Scripture Except Where It Is Impossible To Do So

"If the literal sense makes good sense, seek no other sense, lest it result in nonsense." Unless the passage is *obviously* figurative, it is always to be taken in the plain and literal sense.

" VIII. Always Remember That Every Verse In The Bible Has *Three* Applications

    A. The doctrinal application (often prophetic).

    B. The historical application, meaning the event actually occurred in human history.

    C. The devotional or spiritual application, which is the practical application of the passage to the life and conduct of the believer.

3. REMEMBER: The truth of scripture is revealed to us by the Holy Spirit

> "Now we have received, not the spirit of the world, but the spirit which is of God; that we might know the things that are freely given to us of God.
>
> "Which things also we speak, not in the words which man's wisdom teacheth, but which the Holy Ghost teacheth; comparing spiritual things with spiritual."
>
> **— I Corinthians 2:12-13**

In the context, "comparing spiritual things with spiritual" means comparing scripture with scripture. We are not to compare it even with "the words which man's wisdom teacheth," but with that "which the Holy Ghost teacheth," and that is the word of God.

4. REMEMBER: We are not to believe enticing words, philosophy, deceitful words, traditions of men or the rudiments of the world.[35] Our doctrines are drawn from THE WORDS THEMSELVES.

> "And this I say, lest any man should beguile you with <u>enticing words</u>.
>
> "For though I be absent in the flesh, yet am I with you in the spirit, joying and beholding your order, and the stedfastness of your faith in Christ.
>
> "As ye have therefore received Christ Jesus the Lord, so walk ye in him:
>
> "Rooted and built up in him, and stablished in the faith, as ye have been taught, abounding therein with thanksgiving.
>
> "<u>Beware</u> lest any man spoil you through <u>philosophy and vain deceit, after the tradition of men</u>, after the rudiments of the world, and not after Christ."
>
> **— Colossians 2:4-8**

---

[35] **Rudiment** n. 1. Often rudiments. A fundamental element, principle, or skill, as of a field of learning. 2. Often rudiments. Something in an incipient or undeveloped form: *the rudiments of social behavior in children; the rudiments of a plan of action.* <u>American Heritage Dictionary</u>

"Making <u>the word of God</u> of none effect through your <u>tradition</u>, which ye have delivered: and many such like things do ye."   — Mark 7:13

"Hearken unto me now therefore, O ye children, and attend to <u>the words of my mouth</u>."
— Proverbs 7:24

"All <u>the words of my mouth</u> are in righteousness; there is nothing froward or perverse in them.

"<u>They are all plain</u> to him that understandeth, <u>and right</u> to them that find knowledge."
— Proverbs 8:8-9

"The entrance of thy words giveth light; it giveth understanding unto the simple."   — Psalms 119:130

"Evil men understand not judgment: but they that seek the LORD understand all things."
— Proverbs 28:5

We read in the Holman Bible Handbook

"Asking the Right Questions

"The teacher will examine the text in the framework of the history of God's revelation and in the particular cultural context in which the event occurred. A simple way to approach a story or event is to use the questions any good reporter would ask. The well-known writer Rudyard Kipling wrote that he kept six honest men who served him well and taught him all he knew.

They were:

What? and Why?

When? and How?

Where? and Who?

"These questions serve the teacher or preacher well in the discovery process and can serve well in the teaching or preaching event. The answers can be stated in a positive manner to form the structure of the lesson or sermon.

"A text that is often misinterpreted is Philippians 4:13,

'I can do all things through Christ which strengtheneth me.'

"This verse is often employed to urge people to become
super-Christians in the accomplishment of Herculean tasks.
I have heard preachers suggest that this passage means
that Christians should be able to achieve any goal and live
above the strife of other mortals. If the exegete uses the
reporters questions wisely, this error will likely be avoided.

WHAT? Paul wrote to his friends and
supporters who were concerned
about how he was doing in prison
and about the recent serious illness
of Epaphroditus.

"WHY? He wrote to assure them that he had
not been overwhelmed by difficulties
and that one could survive perilous
conditions through faith.

"WHEN? He wrote while still in prison with the
possibility of execution before him.

"HOW? Faith removes fear and sustains one
in dire circumstances.

"WHERE? The where has been answered and is
important in interpreting the
passage. The fact Paul was in prison
indicated he could not escape persecution and injustice because he was
a Christian. Indeed, his proclamation
of the gospel led to his
imprisonment.

"WHO? The who includes Paul,
Epaphroditus, and all others who

might suffer for the sake of the gospel." [36]

So, we see that this passage does not teach that we can do ALL things. Obviously, you can't fly or jump over a building. There must be a qualifier and it is found in First John chapter five.

"And this is the confidence that we have in him, that, if we ask any thing *according to his will,* he heareth us:"
— **I John 5:14**

Paul could certainly say that where the will of God led him, the grace of God kept him. He was able to bear all things that came upon Him as He served the Lord.

Just like Paul writes to the Corinthian church

"There hath no temptation taken you but such as is common to man: but God is faithful, who will not suffer you to be tempted above that ye are able; but will with the temptation also make a way to escape, that ye may be able to bear it." — **I Corinthians 10:13**

In this manner the true and simple meaning of the text may be seen and applied.

5. REMEMBER: "Scripture" is all Jesus needed to thwart the attack of the Devil in the garden. He said "It is written" [37]

In Matthew we read of the temptation of the Saviour

"Then was Jesus led up of the Spirit into the wilderness to be tempted of the devil."
— **Matthew 4:1**

Three times the Tempter tried to entice the blessed Son of God to sin. And three times our Lord responded, "It is written," because

---

[36] Holman Bible Handbook, (Holman Bible Publishers, Nashville, Tennessee)

[37] We must never forget that we have an enemy, a deceiver who is constantly working to propagate his lies (Matthew 13:38-39; John 8:44; Revelation 12:9).

there was no greater authority He could appeal to than His own word. For He was a king, coming to claim His own.

And, in the words of "the Preacher"

> "Where the word of a king is, there is power…
> — Ecclesiastes 8:4

6. REMEMBER: The Bible is to be trusted above the words of man

> "It is better to trust in the LORD than to put confidence in man."   — Psalms 118:8

> "And they were astonished at his doctrine: for he taught them as one that had <u>authority</u>, and not as the scribes."   — Mark 1:22

> "In the day when God shall judge the secrets of men by Jesus Christ according to <u>my gospel</u>."
> — Romans 2:16

> "He taught me also, and said unto me, Let thine heart retain <u>my words</u>: keep <u>my commandments</u>, and live."   — Proverbs 4:4

> "Ye shall not add unto <u>the word</u> which I command you, neither shall ye diminish ought from it, that ye may keep <u>the commandments</u> of the LORD your God which I command you."   — Deuteronomy 4:2

> "Add thou not unto <u>his words</u>, lest he reprove thee, and thou be found a liar."   — Proverbs 30:6

> "I Jesus have sent mine angel to <u>testify</u> unto you these things in the churches. I am the root and the offspring of David, and the bright and morning star.

> "And the Spirit and the bride say, Come. And let him that heareth say, Come. And let him that is athirst come. And whosoever will, let him take the water of life freely. For I <u>testify</u> unto every man that heareth

the words of the prophecy of this book, If any man shall add unto these things, God shall add unto him the plagues that are written in this book:

"And if any man shall take away from the words of the book of this prophecy, God shall take away his part out of the book of life, and out of the holy city, and from the things which are written in this book."

— Revelation 22:16-19

7. REMEMBER: The word of God is incorruptible and eternal

"Being born again, not of corruptible seed, but of incorruptible, by the word of God, which liveth and abideth for ever." — II Peter 1:23

"We have also a more sure word of prophecy; whereunto ye do well that ye take heed, as unto a light that shineth in a dark place, until the day dawn, and the day star arise in your hearts:

"Knowing this first, that no prophecy of the scripture is of any private interpretation."

— II Peter 1:19-20

8. REMEMBER: The word of God is the power of God

"Jesus answered and said unto them, Ye do err, not knowing the scriptures, nor the power of God."

— Matthew 22:29

9. REMEMBER: The Bible is the inspired word of God

Adrian Moore testifies

"The doctrine of the INERRANT (free from error), INFALLIBLE (incapable of error), INSPIRED (God breathed), Word of God has always been at the forefront of Baptist belief. It must be the FINAL AUTHORITY in faith and practice, for it is GOD'S WORD given to man to reveal Himself and to instruct mankind in the way of salvation through the Lord Jesus Christ. It is the instruction manual in righteousness and can not be superseded by any other set of rules or creeds of man. The dictates of man must never usurp the position of preeminence of the Holy Bible." [38]

I, too, believe that the Bible is the inspired word of God. Therefore, it must follow that it is inerrant and infallible. If not, then its inspiration means nothing. Therefore, we would be left to man to tell us what part of the Bible is the word of God, and what part of the Bible is not the word of God.

C.H. Spurgeon writes

"If THE BOOK be not infallible, where shall we find infallibility? We have given up the Pope, for he has blundered often and terribly; but we shall not set up instead of him a horde of popelings fresh from college. Are these correctors of Scriptures infallible? Is it certain that our Bibles are not right, but that the critics must be so? Now, Farmer Smith, when you have read your Bible, and have enjoyed its precious promises, you will have tomorrow morning, to go down the street to ask the scholarly man at the parsonage whether this portion of the Scripture belongs to the inspired part of the Word or whether it is of dubious authority... We shall gradually be so bedoubted and be criticized that only a few of the most profound will know what is Bible and what is not, and they will dictate to the rest of us. I have no more faith in their mercy than in their accuracy... and we are fully assured that our old English version of the Scriptures is sufficient for plain men for all purposes of life, salvation, and goodness." [39]

What is the FINAL AUTHORITY for the true believer, a fallible Pope or the infallible word of God?

---

[38] **Adrian Moore**, Historic Baptist Distinctives (Lighthouse Baptist Bible Curriculum)

[39] **C.H. Spurgeon**, "The Greatest Fight in the World." This quote is taken from the inaugural address which Spurgeon delivered at the *Pastor's College Conference* in April 1891. Published just before his death, it constitutes Spurgeon's final address to his fellow pastors. Without a doubt it is one of the most forceful sermons that he ever delivered.

As Baptists we have

➲ No *priest,* but Christ

➲ No *sacrifice,* but Calvary

➲ No *confessional,* but the throne of grace

➲ No *authority,* but the word of God.

Scripture teaches us

"But continue thou in the things which thou hast learned and hast been assured of, knowing of whom thou hast learned them;

"And that from a child thou hast known the holy scriptures, which are able to make thee wise unto salvation through faith which is in Christ Jesus.

"All SCRIPTURE is given by INSPIRATION of God, and is profitable for doctrine, for reproof, for correction, for instruction in righteousness:

"That the man of God may be perfect, throughly furnished unto all good works."

— II Timothy 3:14-16

The Hammers and the Anvil

"Last eve I paused before the blacksmith's door
and heard the anvil ring the vesper chime.
And looking in, I saw old hammers on the floor,
Worn by the beating years of time.

"'How many anvils have you had," said I,
'To wear and batter all these hammers so?'
'Just one,' said he, then with a twinkle in his eye,
'The anvil wears the hammers out you know.'

"And so I thought, the anvil of God's word,
For ages skeptic blows have beat upon.
Yet though the noise of falling blows was heard,
The anvil is unharmed— the hammers gone!"

— John Clifford

THROUGHLY FURNISHED

While it is not within the scope of this study to completely cover the doctrine of inspiration, we do want to examine these important verses found in II Timothy 3:14-16.[40] These alone are all that are needed to completely equip (throughly furnish) the child of God to live a life pleasing unto the Lord Jesus Christ who made us, loves, died for us, has gone away to prepare a place for us and is coming again for us.

<u>Paul exhorts Timothy</u>

> **"[C]ontinue thou in the things which thou hast learned and hast been assured of, knowing of whom thou hast learned them."   — II Timothy 3:14**

He told this young preacher to *"continue,"* in what? To continue in *"the holy scriptures"* (vs. 15). Nothing else was recommended, because nothing else was needed.

"[K]nowing of whom thou has learned them," he continues. And of whom had he learned them? — from the Holy Ghost. He is the divine author and instructor who is able to open the scriptures to us, "...through faith, which is in Christ Jesus." Only those "in Christ Jesus" have access to the wonders and mysteries of scripture.

<u>Then, by the inspiration of the Holy Spirit, Paul writes</u>

> **All SCRIPTURE is given by INSPIRATION of God, and is profitable for doctrine, for reproof, for correction, for instruction in righteousness:**
> **— II Timothy 3:16**

---

[40] As "Jehudi's penknife" mutilated the scriptures (Jeremiah 36:23), so modern "scholars" have changed II Timothy 3:14-16 in every English Bible version produced since 1800.

"All scripture is given by inspiration of God..." The question then arises as to *what* Paul means by "scripture." Now, hold up your Bible. Who do you think gave *you* the Bible in your hand? Was it the Catholic church, a team of Protestant scholars, or the Lord Himself? Unregenerate or worldly scholars would be quick to tell us that *"only the originals were inspired."* But is that what Paul said? Not at all; he said A-L-L, "all" *scripture.* So, if you believe the Bible in your hand is "scripture," it was surely given by the Holy Spirit. And though man or devil try to destroy it, the word of God is preserved by God Himself.

T. DeWitt Talmage preached a message from Jeremiah 36

"We look in upon a room in Jerusalem. Two men are there. At the table sits Baruch the scribe, with a roll of parchment and an iron pen in his hand. The other man is walking the floor, as if strangely agitated. There is an unearthly appearance about his countenance, and his whole frame quakes as if pressed upon by something unseen and supernal. It is Jeremiah, in the spirit of prophecy. Being too much excited to write with his own hand the words that the Almighty pours upon his mind about the destruction of Jerusalem, he dictates to Baruch the scribe. It is a seething, scalding, burning denunciation of Jehoiakim, the king, and a prophecy of coming disasters.

"Of course, Jehoiakim the king hears of the occurrence, and he sends Jehudi to obtain the parchment and read its contents. It is winter. Jehoiakim is sitting in his comfortable winter house by a fire that glows upon the hearth, and lights up the faces of the lords, and princes, and senators who have gathered to hear the strange document. Silence is ordered. The royal circle bend forward to listen. Every eye is fixed. Jehudi unrolls the book gleaming with the words of God, and as he reads the king frowns; his eye kindles; his cheek burns; his foot comes down with thundering indignation. He snatches the book from Jehudi's hand, feels for his knife, crumples up the book, and goes to work cutting it up with his penknife.

"Thus God's book was permanently destroyed, and the king escaped. Was it destroyed? Did he escape? In a little while King Jehoiakim's dead body is hurled forth to blacken in the sun, and the only epitaph he ever had was that which Jeremiah wrote: *"Buried with the burial of an ass;"* while, to restore the book which was destroyed, Baruch again takes his seat at the table, and Jeremiah walks the floor and again dictates the terrible prophecy.

"It would take more penknives than cutler ever sharpened to hew into permanent destruction the Word of God. He who shoots at this eternal rock will feel the bullet rebound into his own torn and lacerated bosom. When the Almighty goes forth armed with the thunderbolts of his power, I pity any Jehoiakim who attempts to fight him with a penknife.

"That Oriental scene has vanished, but it has been often repeated. There are thousands of Jehoiakims *yet alive who cut the Word of God with their penknives…*

"No, sir; you shall not rob me of a single word, of a single verse, of a single chapter of a single book of my Bible."[41]

'How precious is the Book divine,
By inspiration given!
Bright as a lamp its doctrines shine
To guide our souls to heaven.

This lamp through all the tedious night
Of life shall guide our way,
Till we behold the clearer light
Of an eternal day.'"

Paul proclaims scripture to be profitable. If the great apostle to the Gentiles was ever given to understatement, this is the place. It is like saying air and water are profitable to your health. Indeed, for without it we could not live.

As Jesus said

"[I]t is written, Man shall not live by bread alone, but by every word that proceedeth out of the mouth of God."   — Matthew 4:4

---

[41] **T. DeWitt Talmage**, "The Reckless Penknife" (1832-1902).

It is given by inspiration of God and therefore no other book can be compared with it. The English word "inspiration" is translated from "theopneustos" in the Greek, and means "God-breathed." In the same way that God breathed into the nostrils of Adam "the breath of life" (Genesis 2:7), He breathed life into the Holy Scriptures.

Jesus said

> **"It is the spirit that quickeneth; the flesh profiteth nothing: the words that I speak unto you, they are spirit, and they are life."　　　— John 6:63**

The word "spirit" (pneuma) is from the same Greek root as "pneustos" in "theopneustos." In the Greek language, *pneuma* means wind or breath.[42] You may be familiar with other words that come from this root, like *pneumatic drill* (driven by compressed air), and *pneumonia* (an illness that affects the lungs; your breath). The *breath of God* is His Spirit (Job 33:4). Therefore the word of God is a *living* book. If it were not, then it could not give life; and we know that life ONLY comes from some other living thing.

> **"Being born again, not of corruptible seed, but of incorruptible, by the word of God, which liveth and abideth for ever."　　　— I Peter 1:23**

> **"For the word of God is quick, and powerful, and sharper than any twoedged sword, piercing even to the dividing asunder of soul and spirit, and of the joints and marrow, and is a discerner of the thoughts and intents of the heart."　　　— Hebrews 4:12**

In Hebrews 4:12, the word "quick," means "alive." Think about that. That is an extraordinary book I hold in my hand; it is alive! And wonder of wonders, it has the power to give eternal life to all who believe it, by faith.

---

[42] **W.E. Vine**, <u>An Expository Dictionary of New Testament Words</u>, (Fleming Revell)

Dr. Peter S. Ruckman writes

"The Holy Spirit not only inspired the original autographs, but the scriptures we have in our hands (a *King James 1611 Authorized Version* of the Bible). And by the way, the term *'scripture'* in the Bible is never a reference to the *original manuscripts.*" [43]

"Now, the primary purpose for the writing of the scripture— according to the Holy Spirit who wrote the scripture— was doctrine. II Timothy 3:16 says, *'All scripture is given by inspiration of God, and is profitable for doctrine...'* Paul told Timothy to labor in doctrine and that an elder who labored in doctrine was worthy of double honor (I Timothy 5:17). He also said that Timothy could save his own ministry and save the testimony of the people who heard him if he spent time and gave attention to doctrine (I Timothy 4:13-16). **Sound doctrine** is the absolute essential quality in the last day in the Laodicean church and is the last thing the modern Laodicean Christian wants to fool with because it is divisive and controversial." [44]

Scripture Is Profitable For Doctrine

Of all the things we want to learn from the word of God, doctrine is the most important. *("Doctrine"* simply means the things that the Bible teaches about a certain subject.) There are over 5,000 different denominations in the United States today, each one having a different interpretation of the scriptures. Members of these denominations strictly adhere to the teaching of their own peculiar sect; but in our study, we are interested in what *the word of God* teaches, because it is the only pure source of doctrine we will ever study. We must set our hearts upon learning *what the Bible **says**,* and *not* what a man or a denomination believes. The only way we will ever know the truth is to take the scriptures in the *1611 Authorized Version* at face value. ***The Final***

---

[43] **Peter S. Ruckman,** Theological Studies • Book 12 • The Work of the Holy Spirit, Page 7.

[44] **Peter S. Ruckman,** Theological Studies • Book 11 • The Deity and Names of the Holy Spirit

Authority for the believer, above what anyone teaches, the faithful standard by which we may judge all things, is the King James Bible.

David wrote:

> "Thy word is very pure: therefore thy servant loveth it."   — Psalm 119:140

As we read in the book of Romans:

> "Let God be true, but every man a liar."
> — Romans 3:4

The Psalms also warn us:

> "It is better to trust in the Lord than to put confidence in man."   — Psalm 118:8

Scripture Is Profitable For Reproof

In II Timothy 3:16, *"reproof"* implies the exposing of error and conviction of sin, with a suggestion of shame upon the one convicted. Scripture can be very pointed about our sin, but it is always for our good and in preparation of the *remedy*. The purpose of pointing out our sin is that we might receive correction and instruction. Some things may be hidden from men; but scripture is the light that uncovers all things, for nothing is hidden from God.

> "Thy word is a lamp unto my feet, and a light unto my path."   — Psalm 119:105

> "All things that are reproved are made manifest by the light: for whatsoever doth make manifest is light."
> — Ephesians 5:13

> "For everyone that doeth evil hateth the light, neither cometh to the light, lest his deeds should be reproved."   — John 3:20

Once reproved, we should heed the warning of Proverbs 29:

> "He, that being often reproved hardeneth his neck,
> shall suddenly be destroyed, and that without
> remedy."   — Proverbs 29:1

Let us not be as this man, but accept the reproof of the scriptures as a kindness from the Lord, and the attending correction with joy.

Scripture Is Profitable For Correction

Correction is the *remedy* that will lead us to the restoration of our relationship with the Lord after we have sinned. In the scriptures, chastening is closely linked to correction.

> "Behold happy is the man whom God correcteth:
> therefore despise not the chastening of the
> Almighty."   — Job 5:17

> "My son, despise not the chastening of the Lord;
> neither be weary of his correction.
> "For whom the LORD loveth he correcteth; even as
> a father the son in whom he delighteth."
>
>   — Proverbs 3:11-12

And we know

> "[N]o chastening for the present seemeth to be
> joyous, but grievous: nevertheless afterward it
> yieldeth the peaceable fruit of righteousness unto
> them that are exercised thereby."   — Hebrews 12:11

Scripture Is Profitable For Instruction

The Bible never leads anyone to do wrong; it always instructs us to do right. It is not even necessary that we understand everything in the scriptures in order to profit by them; but it is necessary that we believe them. We know that by and by the Holy Spirit will give understanding to the man who believes what God said.

Paul expressed his desire for all believers in this regard.

> **"For this cause also, since the day we heard it, do not cease to pray for you, and to desire that you might be filled with the knowledge of his will in all wisdom and spiritual understanding;"**
> **— Colossians 1:9**

The Bible teaches us how to live a life that is pleasing unto the Lord. However, we must study the word of God and give attendance to the teaching and preaching of it. Thereby we can learn the great doctrines of the faith. Studying the scriptures will help perfect us and thoroughly furnish us unto all good works.

What Martin Luther said hundreds of years ago still holds true:

> "In truth, you cannot read the scriptures too much;
>
> What you read, you cannot too well read;
>
> What you read well, you cannot too well understand;
>
> What you understand well, you cannot too well teach;
>
> And what you teach well, you cannot too well live."

W.A. Criswell gives this simple illustration

> "Washington, DC, is the home of the Bureau of Standards. Every weight and every measure that is used in the United States is a copy of the standard that is kept inviolate by the bureau in Washington. In that bureau, there is a perfect inch, a perfect foot, a perfect yard, a perfect gallon, a perfect pint, a perfect millimeter, a perfect milligram. Every weight and measure that we have finds its standard in that bureau in Washington, and all are judged by that standard." [45]

A solid foundation is essential to any belief. Like a building, it must be on unshakable ground. This was illustrated when a major power company was erecting a nuclear power plant. Millions of

---

[45] **W.A. Criswell**, The Bible for Today's World

dollars were spent on the massive structure that would house the nuclear reactor. But inspection showed the foundations to be inadequate. As a result, the safety of the community was uncertain and the project had to be abandoned.

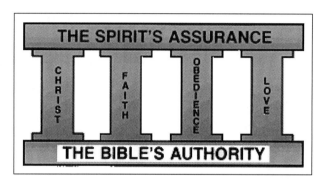

Dr. Peter S. Ruckman graphically sums it up

"God's final showdown with Conservatives, Fundamentalists, and Evangelicals at the end of the Laodicean Church period (Revelation 3) will have to do with the controversy over the authority of the *Authorized Version.* Consequently, apostate Fundamentalists, between 1950 and 1980, have been trying desperately to renew old arguments about "the fundamentals" being the real issue; a few Post-tribulation rapturists have been trying to make an issue out of whether or not the Church will go through the Tribulation. But all attempts to sidetrack the Body of Christ from its terrible duty (and its true obligation) have failed and will continue to fail. The disturbing fact remains that the church in the twentieth century, having argued (thoroughly) all the major doctrines in the Bible and having defined what a Christian is supposed to believe concerning them (Trinitarian controversies in the first and second centuries, the natures of Christ in the third and fourth centuries, the problem of the sacraments, the authority of bishops, etc.), has finally arrived in this last century at the jumping-off place: Is THE BOOK from which she received her 'doctrines' true, or is it *not?*"[46]

---

[46] **Peter S. Ruckman,** The "Errors" in the King James Bible (previously titled Problem Texts)

WE ARE BIBLE-BELIEVING BAPTISTS, WHO BELIEVE THAT THE FINAL AUTHORITY FOR ALL WE BELIEVE AND PRACTICE LIES IN ONE BOOK; THE KING JAMES BIBLE.

Here Is A Timeless Warning From C.H. Spurgeon

"Every MOTIVE that could move men to alter the Word of God has been fully delineated in various portions of the Bible. It shows that God was aware from the first of the reception that would be given to His truth; and it is as instructing to the humble believer as it is humiliating to the modern lover of penknife criticism.

"The TENDENCY to alter the Word of God is HUMAN. It is manifested in the first religious conversation on record. The Divine voice had asserted 'Thou shalt not eat of it;' the human voice added 'neither shall ye touch it.' The addition was the precursor of the fall.

"The DESIRE to alter the Word of God is DANGEROUS. In the wilderness God Himself points this out. 'Ye shall not add unto the Word which I command you, neither shall ye diminish ought from it' (Deuteronomy 4:2). The nations they were advancing to conquer had long cast aside their allegiance to their Maker, and the least tendency to question or alter God's Word might result in the same downfall for Israel. 'Thou shalt not add thereto, nor diminish from it.' That idolatry does result from such daring rebellion is proved by the state of the Roman Catholic community today.

"The ACT of altering the Word of God is SINFUL. 'Add not unto His words, lest He reprove thee, and thou be found a liar' (Proverbs 30:5-6) 'Every word of God is pure;' and he who essays to improve upon it imputes error to the All-wise. Only unholy minds could attempt it.

"The DESIRE to alter the Word of God is WEAKNESS. Jeremiah's was a terrible message, and even he might yield to feelings of pity for his race. God saw this, and in words that could not be misunderstood, He said to the prophet, 'Diminish not a word' (Jeremiah 26:2). If God's message is diminished its power is lessened, and its results are consequently less certain. The authority, the power, the meaning, the terror of God's truth must be preserved in all their fulness if God's purposes are to be carried out.

"The AMBITION to alter the Word of God is PHARISAIC. To break the perfection of the law and teach our own alterations or additions as if they were of God is vile indeed (Matthew 5:19,20). Our Lord reproved this spirit in scathing and unmistakable language. Why is it His Words are forgotten? 'Ye have made the commandment of God of none effect by your tradition,' He says. 'They teach for doctrines the commandments of men' (Matthew 15:6-9). The Pharisaic spirit thus renders impossible, obedience to God, the Supreme Teacher.

"The CRAVING to alter the Word of God is ACCURSED. Revelation 22:18-19 should be read with fear and trembling. Thus all down the ages God has warned men against this crime. He is a jealous God, and has determined to visit with the direst punishment all who dare to alter His completed and full revelation.

"This is the crime of the present day: the Lord preserve us from it."

M.R. DeHaan wrote

"Be on guard against any tampering with the Word, whether disguised as a search for truth, or a scholarly attempt at apparently hidden meanings; and beware of the confusion created by the senseless rash of new versions, translations, editions, and improvements upon the tried and tested Bible of our fathers and grandfathers."[47]

Horatius Bonar wrote

"Let the Bible be to us the one book in all the world, whose every word is truth, and whose every verse is wisdom. In studying it, be sure to take it for what it really is,

---

[47] **M.R. DeHaan**, Portraits of Christ in Genesis, (Kregel Publications) 1995, DeHaan was an American Bible teacher and physician (1891-1965).

the revelation of the thoughts of God given us in the words of God. Were it only the book of divine thoughts and human words, it would profit little, for we never could be sure whether the words really represented the thoughts; nay, we might be sure that man would fail in his words when attempting to embody divine thoughts; and that, therefore, if we have only man's words, that is man's translation of the divine thoughts.

"But, knowing that we have divine thoughts embodied in divine words through the inspiration of an unerring translator, we sit down to the study of the heavenly volume, assured that we shall find in all its teachings the perfection of wisdom, and in its language the most accurate expression of that wisdom that the finite speech of man could utter."[48]

J.C. Ryle made this observation

"It is hard enough to fight the devil, the world and the flesh, without private differences in our own camp. But there is one thing that is even worse than controversy, and that is false doctrine tolerated... and permitted ...There are times when controversy is not only a duty but also a benefit, and it is a plain scriptural duty to *'contend earnestly for the faith once delivered to the saints.'*

"The apostle Paul... was beaten with rods, stoned and left for dead, chained and left in a dungeon, dragged before magistrates, barely escaped assassination, and so pronounced in him were [his convictions] that it came to a point when the unbelieving Jews of Thessalonica declared: *'These that have turned the world upside down are come hither also.'*

"God pity those pastors and Christian leaders whose main objective is the growth of their organizations and whose main concern is lest their 'boats be rocked.' THEY MAY ESCAPE CONTROVERSY, BUT THEY WILL NOT ESCAPE THE JUDGMENT SEAT OF CHRIST."[49]

---

[48] **Horatius Bonar**, Follow the Lamb, (R. Carter and Brothers), 1874

[49] **J.C. Ryle**, Warning to the Churches, (Banner of Truth) December 1, 1967

PART TWO

AUTONOMY
OF CHURCHES

AUTONOMY OF CHURCHES

The word "autonomous" comes from the Greek word "autos" (meaning "self") and "nomos" (meaning "law" or "rule"). It refers to the power and right of self government.

The American Heritage Dictionary defines "autonomy:"

> "The capacity to manage one's affairs and make decisions: independence, autonomy, freedom, liberty, self-determination, self-reliance, self-rule."[50]

Edward Hisox says

> "Baptists assert that each particular local Church is self-governing, and independent of all other churches, and of all persons and bodies of men whatever, as to the administration of its own affairs; that it is of right and should be, free from any other human authority, whether civil or ecclesiastical, and that this is the New Testament idea of church government."[51]

We encourage cooperation with other Bible-believing independent Baptist churches. However, even then, one church is not to exercise control over another. Each local assembly is to stand before God as an independent entity and is responsible for its own actions. The local church is to call its own pastor, carry out its own discipline, administrate (for that local assembly) the statutes of the Word of God and endeavor to serve the Lord as guided by the Holy Spirit. Of course, when a new church is begun as a mission work, there is a time when it is under the authority of a missionary.

Today this view of the autonomy is being challenged in every country around the world. Therefore, there is a serious question

---

[50] American Heritage Dictionary

[51] **Edward T. Hiscox**, The New Directory for Baptist Churches (1859)

that Christians around the world must come to grips with: Who has the authority to rule over the affairs of the church of God on earth? Of course, if I were to ask the question *"Who has the authority to rule over the affairs of the church in heaven?"* the answer would be quite apparent, since the only government in heaven is God's government. But *if* there is a God, His authority is supreme not only in heaven, but in all of His creation.

George Truett, in his 1939 address to the *Baptist World Alliance*, said:

"For any person or institution to dare to come between the soul and God is a blasphemous impertinence.' [52]

Consider the following scriptures:

"In the beginning God created the heaven and the earth."   — Genesis 1:1

"Know ye that the LORD he is God: *it is he that hath made us,* and not we ourselves..."
— Psalm 100:3

"Thine, O LORD, is the greatness, and the power, and the glory, and the victory, and the majesty: for all that is in the heaven and in the earth is thine; thine is the kingdom, O LORD, and *thou art exalted as head above all.*"   — I Chronicles 29:11

"And to make all men see what is the fellowship of the mystery, which from the beginning of the world hath been hid in God, *who created all things by Jesus Christ:*"   — Ephesians 3:9

"And Jesus came and spake unto them, saying, *All power is given unto me in heaven and in earth.*"
— Matthew 28:18

---

[52] Quoted by **J.M. Dawson** in Baptists and the American Republic (Broadman, 1956) p. 221.

> "A Psalm of David. *The earth is the LORD'S,* and the fulness thereof; the world, and they that dwell therein."   — Psalm 24:1

Paul wrote to the Ephesian church:

> "[T]hat ye may know...
>
> "...the exceeding greatness of his power
>
> "Which he wrought in Christ, when he raised him from the dead, and set him at his own right hand in the heavenly places,
>
> "Far above all principality, and power, and might, and dominion, and every name that is named, not only in this world, but also in that which is to come:
>
> "And hath put all things under his feet, and gave him to be the head over all things to the church,"
>
>   — Ephesians 1:19-22

The scripture clearly shows that God has made all things and He has the power and authority, of Himself, to rule over all the things He has made. Now, the Lord Jesus Christ is *"above all principality, and power, and might, and dominion, and every name that is named, not only in this world, but also in that which is to come."* Furthermore, all things are *"under his feet"* and he is *"the head over all things to the church."* Therefore, the answer to this question of authority is quite elementary to the Bible-believing Christian whose answer comes, not from some man or some carnal philosophy, but from the living word of God. Since the Holy Bible is the absolute and final authority above anything we think or believe, we must know what it teaches about this critical issue.

We believe the Bible teaches that God established three institutions on earth.

I quote a well known Baptist pastor.

> "We note that **the church is independent of the state**. Baptists have always contended for this biblical principle. It will help to remember that **the Lord established three great institutions: the HOME, the GOVERNMENT, and the** CHURCH. We have responsibilities toward each one,

and there is an interdependency in their relationship toward each other. Yet each one is sovereign in its own field. Christians are to **obey** civil rulers (Romans 13), recognizing that the Lord ordained government and granted to men the ultimate authority of capital punishment (Genesis 9:6; Romans 13:4). We are also to **pray** for civil rulers (I Timothy 2:1,2); and we are to **pay** our taxes (Matthew 22:21; Romans 13:6,7). The church, in turn, has a right to the protection of civil law as the government deals with evildoers. However, the church has no instructions concerning the administration of civil affairs, **nor does the word of God ever permit the state to interfere in the conduct of spiritual things.**"[53]

That summarizes the issue pretty well. Now let's examine the subject in detail.

God Established Religious Worship

From the beginning, God instructed man in the proper manner of worship. Worship is strictly a matter between God and the individual. In the Garden of Eden, man communed with the Lord daily. But the day Adam sinned, he died spiritually and was separated from God. After the expulsion from the Garden of Eden, God established a relationship with man based on worship, offerings, and sacrifices. This became the responsibility of each household, **corporately** (led by the head of the household), and of each person, **individually**. The oldest account of this is found in the Book of Genesis and the Book of Job.

> **"And in process of time it came to pass, that Cain brought of the fruit of the ground an offering unto the LORD.**
>
> **"And Abel, he also brought of the firstlings of his flock and of the fat thereof. And the LORD had respect unto Abel and to his offering:**

---

[53] **Paul Jackson**, The Doctrine and Administration of the Church, (Regular Baptist Press) p. 36

"But unto Cain and to his offering he had not respect. And Cain was very wroth, and his countenance fell.

"And the LORD said unto Cain, Why art thou wroth? and why is thy countenance fallen?

"If thou doest well, shalt thou not be accepted? and if thou doest not well, sin lieth at the door. And unto thee shall be his desire, and thou shalt rule over him.

"And Cain talked with Abel his brother: and it came to pass, when they were in the field, that Cain rose up against Abel his brother, and slew him."

— Genesis 4:3-8

Abel obeyed God in respect to proper worship and sacrifice, and was blessed. Cain, on the other hand, did not bring the proper sacrifice, but thought his own way of worshipping God would be just as good. Cain found that man does not have the authority to change that which God has established, and he cannot worship God in his own way. In order to be pleasing to God, proper worship must be given according to God's word. Notice that Cain rebelled against the Lord and took vengeance against his own brother, because he refused to submit to God's authority.

"By faith Abel offered unto God a more excellent *sacrifice* than Cain, by which he obtained witness that he was righteous,"   — Hebrews 11:4

Again we see *sacrifices* being offered in the Book of Job.

"And it was so, when the days of their feasting were gone about, that Job sent and sanctified them, and rose up early in the morning, and offered burnt offerings according to the number of them all: for Job said, It may be that my sons have sinned, and cursed God in their hearts. Thus did Job continually."

— Job 1:5

We do not offer sacrifices today, since the Lord Jesus Christ became our sacrifice, once for ever.

"Wherefore he is able also to save them to the uttermost that come unto God by him, seeing he ever liveth to make intercession for them.

"For such an high priest became us, who is holy, harmless, undefiled, separate from sinners, and made higher than the heavens;

"Who needeth not daily, as those high priests, to offer up sacrifice, first for his own sins, and then for the people's: for this he did once, when he offered up himself."

— Hebrews 7:25-27

"For Christ is not entered into the holy places made with hands, which are the figures of the true; but into heaven itself, now to appear in the presence of God for us:

"Nor yet that he should offer himself often, as the high priest entereth into the holy place every year with blood of others;

"For then must he often have suffered since the foundation of the world: but now once in the end of the world hath he appeared to put away sin by the sacrifice of himself.

"And as it is appointed unto men once to die, but after this the judgment:

"So Christ was once offered to bear the sins of many; and unto them that look for him shall he appear the second time without sin unto salvation."

— Hebrews 9:24-28

These passages of scripture show that God established worship, offerings and sacrifices whereby man could go to God. Because our Savior offered Himself for our sins, the holiest is now opened to every believer. We may now worship him privately and individually and that worship is based upon a personal relationship between God and man; a relationship that kings and government have no part therein.

Who Established The Church?

The Lord Jesus Christ Himself founded the Church that is the body of Christ, even as He created the heavens and the earth— by the Holy Spirit. Furthermore, He continues to rule the Church by His Spirit to this day. After the New Testament was established in His blood (cf. Luke 22:20), all things were ready and waiting only for the coming of the Holy Spirit to inaugurate it on the day of Pentecost.

> **"How much more shall the blood of Christ, who through the eternal Spirit offered himself without spot to God, purge your conscience from dead works to serve the living God?**
>
> **"And for this cause he is the mediator of the new testament, that by means of death, for the redemption of the transgressions that were under the first testament, they which are called might receive the promise of eternal inheritance.**
>
> **"For where a testament is, there must also of necessity be the death of the testator."**
>
> **— Hebrews 9:14-16**

However, there still remained the fulfillment of His promise to send the Holy Spirit.

In so doing, it was necessary that the Lord Jesus Christ:

1. Immediately **regenerate** them (Ephesians 2:1; II Corinthians 5:17)

2. Spiritually **baptize** them (Acts 1:5; I Corinthians 12:13; Romans 6:3; Galatians 3:27),

3. Permanently **indwell** them (John 14:17),

4. Securely **seal** them (II Corinthians 1:22; Eph. 1:13; 4:30),

5. Spiritually **circumcise** them (Colossians 2:11,12)

6. Fill and **empower** them (Acts 1:8; 2:4).

All this was done with the Holy Ghost in placing them into the *body of Christ;* none of these things could have been accomplished before the New Testament was established *in His blood* (Hebrews 9:14). Therefore, the New Testament Church was birthed at the time of the feast of Pentecost, as recorded in Acts chapter two.

Here, let me emphasize that the Church (though often called an *organization*) is actually a *living organism,* made up of *living stones* (I Peter 2:5) and having a *living head.* Furthermore, one becomes part of this *spiritual organism,* only by spiritual birth (John 3:3, 7; I Peter 1:23). In addition, members of the one spiritual Body are directed to associate themselves together in local assemblies (I Corinthians 11:18, 20; Hebrews 10:25).

Who Has The Authority To Rule The Church?

Jesus Christ is the Head of the New Testament church, the body of Christ. Men alone cannot properly rule it without the direct guidance of the Savior who is that head.

"Which he wrought in Christ, when he raised him from the dead, and set him at his own right hand in the heavenly places,

"Far above all principality, and power, and might, and dominion, and every name that is named, not only in this world, but also in that which is to come:

"And hath put all things under his feet, and gave him to be the head over all things to the church,

"Which is his body, the fulness of him that filleth all in all."
— Ephesians 1:20-23

"For the husband is the head of the wife, even as Christ is the head of the church: and he is the saviour of the body."   — Ephesians 5:23

"Who hath delivered us from the power of darkness, and hath translated us into the kingdom of his dear Son:

"In whom we have redemption through his blood, even the forgiveness of sins:

"Who is the image of the invisible God, the first-born of every creature:

"For by him were all things created, that are in heaven, and that are in earth, visible and invisible, whether they be thrones, or dominions, or principalities, or powers: all things were created by him, and for him:

"And he is before all things, and by him all things consist.

"And he is the head of the body, the church: who is the beginning, the firstborn from the dead; that in all things he might have the preeminence."

— Colossians 1:13-18

In I Peter 2:25 the Lord Jesus Christ is referred to as the *"Shepherd"* and *"Bishop"* of our souls. In I Peter 5:4 He is called the *"Chief Shepherd"* in a context which makes Him the true Pastor of every believer, in every church. What a wonderful consolation to know that He personally cares for His own.

As Paul wrote

"Now our Lord Jesus Christ himself, and God, even our Father, which hath loved us, and hath given us everlasting consolation and good hope through grace,

"Comfort your hearts, and stablish you in every good word and work."

— II Thessalonians 2:16-17

Therefore, led by His Spirit, the bishop/pastor, is to rule his flock in the Spirit that the Chief Shepherd rules over the entire Body of Christ.

A necessary factor in organization is *leadership*. This is exhibited in the many forms of worldly organizations: An army needs officers; a sporting team needs a captain; a business needs management, etc. In each case, the body concerned may function, but certainly not as well or efficiently as it would with good leadership. In the same way, a church will only be able to serve God if it has God-given leadership.

In God's chain of command, scriptural leadership brings order out of confusion. When sin first entered in, God put the man over the woman to restore order in a state of chaos (Genesis 3:16; I Corinthians 11:3). God placed parents in a position of authority over their children to ensure orderly development, (Exodus 20;12; Psalm 58:3; Proverbs 22:6). God ordained human government to prevent anarchy, (Judges 21:25; Romans 13:1-7). In the same way the Lord has set pastors over His churches to "set in order" things that may be wanting (Titus 1:5).

Scriptural church government places **elders** in the position of *oversight* (Acts 20:17, 28), *leadership* (Ephesians 4:11), and *rulership* (Hebrews 13:7, 17) over the congregation. Pastoral leadership is an integral part of Baptist church government.

<u>Now, let's take a look at the different forms of church government</u>

"EPISCOPAL

"The name episcopal comes from the Greek word *'episkopos',* meaning 'overseer' (the word is also translated "bishop" in the KJV), and identifies churches governed by the authority of bishops. Different denominations are identified by episcopal government, the simplest form being the Methodist church. More complex structure is found in the Episcopal (Anglican) church. The most complex episcopal structure is found in the Roman Catholic church, with the ultimate authority vested in the bishop of Rome, the Pope. The Lutheran church also follows the episcopal form.

"In the episcopal form of church government the authority rests with the bishops who oversee not one church, but a group of churches. Inherent in the office of bishop is the power to ordain ministers or priests. Roman Catholics suggest this authority is derived through apostolic succession from the original apostles. They claim this authority on the basis of Matthew 16:18-19. Others, such as the Methodists, do not acknowledge authority through apostolic succession.

"This form of government arose in the second century, but adherents would claim biblical support from the position of James in the church of Jerusalem, as well as the position and authority of Timothy and Titus.

"PRESBYTERIAN

"The name 'presbyterian' comes from the Greek word 'presbuteros,' meaning 'elder,' and suggests the dignity, maturity, and age of the church leaders. Presbyterian (sometimes termed federal) designates a church government that is governed by elders as in the Presbyterian and Reformed churches. In contrast to the congregational form of government, the presbyterian form emphasizes representative rule by the elders who are appointed or elected by the people. The session, which is made up of elected ruling elders (the teaching elder presiding over it), governs the local church. Above the session is the presbytery, including all ordained ministers or teaching elders as well as one ruling elder from each local congregation in a district. 'Above the presbytery is the synod, and over the synod is the general assembly, the highest court. Both of these bodies are also equally divided between ministers and laymen or ruling elders.' The pastor serves as one of the elders.

"The biblical support for this is the frequent mention of elders in the New Testament: there were elders in Jerusalem (Acts 11:30; 15:2,4) and in Ephesus (Acts 20:17); elders were appointed in every church (Acts 14:23; Titus. 1:5); elders were responsible to feed the flock (I Peter 5:1, 2); there were also elders who ruled (I Timothy 5:17).

"CONGREGATIONAL

"In congregational church government the authority rests not with a representative individual but with the entire local congregation. Two things are stressed in a congregational governed church: autonomy and democracy. A congregational church is autonomous in that no authority outside of the local church has any power over the local church. In addition, congregational churches are democratic in their government; all the members of the local congregation make the decisions that guide and govern the church. This is particularly argued from the standpoint of the priesthood of all believers. Baptists, Evangelical Free, Congregational, some Lutherans, and some independent churches follow the congregational form of church government.

"The biblical support for congregational church government is that the congregation was involved in electing the deacons (Acts 6:3-5) and elders (Acts 14:23); the entire church sent out Barnabas (Acts 11:22) and Titus (II Corinthians 8:19) and received Paul and Barnabas (Acts 14:27; 15:4); the entire church was involved in the decisions concerning circumcision (Acts 15:25); discipline was carried out by the entire church (I Corinthians 5:12; II Corinthians 2:6-7; II Thessalonians 3:14); all believers are responsible for correct doctrine by testing the spirits (I John 4:1), which they are able to do since they have the anointing (I John 2:20)." [54]

'CONGREGATIONAL GOVERNMENT

A. Description
1. *Authority*
Basically the congregational form of government means that ultimate authority for governing the church rests in the members themselves.

2. *Autonomy*
Additionally, it also means that each individual church is an autonomous unit with no individual or organization above it, except Christ the Head.

3. *Responsibility*
Congregationalism does not imply that the entire congregation votes on every decision. Responsibility is delegated to officials and leaders, though, like other members, they have only one vote in the congregation.

4. *Fellowship*
Neither does it mean that churches are so autonomous that they have no fellowship with each other.

---

[54] **Paul P. Enns**, Moody Handbook of Theology (Moody Press, Chicago, Illinois)

B. Support

   1. *Local Autonomy*
   Though the apostles and their delegates did exercise authority over more than one local church, elders and deacons in New Testament times did not. Therefore, today, since apostles have passed off the scene, local churches are autonomous.

   2. *Discipline*
   The whole church was empowered to exercise discipline (Matthew 18:17; I Corinthians 5:4; II Corinthians 2:6-7; II Thessalonians 3:14-15). Since the important matter of discipline was not committed to the leaders only but to the whole congregation, this supports the concept of congregational government.

   3. *Leadership*
   The whole church was involved in choosing leaders. Certain passages clearly support this (Acts 1:23, 26; 6:3, 5; 15:22, 30; II Corinthians 8:19). Others, like Acts 14:23 and Titus 1:5, seem to argue against congregational involvement in choosing. Acts 14:23 records the appointing of leaders on the return leg of the first missionary journey. The verb cheirotoneo does mean appoint, though congregationalists would prefer a more etymologically related understanding of the verb as indicating a choice by raising the hands; that is, a congregational vote. However, even congregationalist Baptist theologian A.H. Strong recognizes that the idea of a popular vote cannot be sustained by the verb. He negates the use of this verse as well as Titus 1:5 (where Titus was instructed to appoint elders in every city) to support the federal type of government by stating that the verses "decide nothing as to the mode of choice, nor is a choice by the community thereby necessarily excluded" (Systematic Theology [Philadelphia: Judson, 1907], p. 906). It might be better for the congregationalist

simply to acknowledge these examples as apostolic and not instructive for us today.

4. *Ordinances*
Several passages commit the ordinances to the whole church, not simply to the leaders or to a hierarchy (Matthew 28:19-20; I Corinthians 11:2, 20).

5. *Government*
The priesthood of all believers argues for a democratic, congregational concept of government (I Peter 2:5, 9).

C. An Appraisal of Congregationalism

1. *Authority*
That ultimate authority rests in the local church under Christ's headship does seem to be clearly taught in the New Testament. This does not preclude fellowship with other congregations, but it does not allow for organizational structure above the local church.

2. *Choosing leaders*
That the whole church was involved in many of the affairs of the congregation also seems clear. But it was not involved in everything. In some instances leaders were clearly appointed and not voted on by everyone. The choosing of the first nonapostolic helpers in Acts 6 exemplifies a gracious harmony between the apostles who asked the congregation to choose and the congregation which placed their choices before the apostles for ratification. We are not told what would have happened had the congregation chosen someone the apostles did not approve of. Presumably such a person would not have been allowed to serve (which means that the congregation was not the final authority).

3. *Restrictions*
Sometimes there seems to be a subtle but consequential blurring of the distinction between what all believers possess equally as members of the body of Christ and what all believers can do as far as ministry within that body is concerned. Because it is true that all believers are priests does not mean that all believers can function in the same offices. The qualifications for leadership do exclude some. To cite an analogy, though all adult United States citizens can vote, not all can be members of Congress (they must have reached a certain age) and not all can be President (he must be a natural-born citizen). While there is a democratic base, there are restrictions which eliminate some citizens from certain activities. So it seems equally true in the church, and congregationalism may consciously or unconsciously sublimate this.

4. *Plurality of leadership*
In practice, congregationalism is not fully congregational. The congregation does not make all the decisions. Leaders do take authority that is not always specifically given to them. The deacons often function like elders so that in effect there is a plurality of leadership. Actually some congregational and federal churches function very similarly. This is especially true when the federally governed church is autonomous. If it is part of a denomination, then it differs clearly from the autonomous congregational church."[55]

We believe the "congregational" system of church government is the biblical system. This means the church is self governing and appoints its own leaders according to the scriptural offices mentioned in the Bible (see chapter on Two Offices).

---

[55] **Charles C. Ryrie**, <u>Basic Theology</u> (Victor Books)

PART THREE

PRIESTHOOD OF THE BELIEVER

PREFACE

The best preface for this chapter that I could imagine is the preface to another book written sixty years ago by A.W. Tozer. Unfortunately, few took it to heart, and the church has greatly suffered for ignoring the clarion call of this prophet of God. It should cause all spiritually minded men to tremble in shame and fear that, after sixty years, these words are more true than ever; yet the warning remains unheeded. As individuals, we make up the New Testament priesthood of believers. We must therefore judge ourselves and draw nigh unto God individually, then the Holy Spirit will move among the Church so that we can truly bear the light of Christ before a lost and dying world.

Bro. Tozer wrote:

"In This Hour Of All-But-Universal darkness, one cheering gleam appears: within the fold of conservative Christianity there are to be found increasing numbers of persons whose religious lives are marked by a growing hunger after God Himself. They are eager for spiritual realities and will not be put off with words, nor will they be content with correct 'interpretations' of truth. They are athirst for God, and they will not be satisfied till they have drunk deep at the Fountain of Living Water.

"This is the only real harbinger of revival which I have been able to detect anywhere on the religious horizon. It may be the cloud the size of a man's hand for which a few saints here and there have been looking. It can result in a resurrection of life for many souls and a recapture of that radiant wonder which should accompany faith in Christ, that wonder which has all but fled the Church of God in our day.

"But this hunger must be recognized by our religious leaders. Current evangelicalism has (to change the figure) laid the altar and divided the sacrifice into parts, but now seems satisfied to count the stones and rearrange the pieces with never a care that there is not a sign of fire upon the top of lofty Carmel. But God be thanked that there are a few who care. They are those who, while they love the altar and delight in the sacrifice, are yet unable to reconcile themselves to the continued absence of fire. They desire God above all. They are athirst to taste for themselves the 'piercing sweetness' of the love of Christ about Whom all the holy prophets did write and the psalmists did sing.

"There is today no lack of Bible teachers to set forth correctly the principles of the doctrines of Christ, but too many of these seem satisfied to teach the fundamentals of the faith year after year, strangely unaware that there is in their ministry no manifest Presence, nor anything unusual in their personal lives. They minister constantly to believers who feel within their breasts a longing which their teaching simply does not satisfy.

"I trust I speak in charity, but the lack in our pulpits is real. Milton's terrible sentence applies to our day as accurately as it did to his: 'The hungry sheep look up, and are not fed.' It is a solemn thing, and no small scandal in the Kingdom, to see God's children starving while actually seated at the Father's table. The truth of Wesley's words is established before our eyes: 'Orthodoxy, or right opinion, is, at best, a very slender part of religion. Though right tempers cannot subsist without right opinions, yet right opinions may subsist without right tempers. There may be a right opinion of God without either love or one right temper toward Him. Satan is a proof of this.'

"Thanks to our splendid Bible societies and to other effective agencies for dissemination of the Word, there are today many millions of people who hold 'right opinions,' probably more than ever before in the history of the Church. Yet I wonder if there was ever a time when true spiritual worship was at a lower ebb. To great sections of the Church the art of worship has been lost entirely, and in its place has come that strange and foreign thing called the 'program.' This word has been borrowed from the stage and applied with sad wisdom to the type of public service which now passes for worship among us.

"Sound Bible exposition is an imperative must in the Church of the Living God. Without it no church can be a New Testament church in any strict meaning of that term. But exposition may be carried on in such a way as to leave the hearers devoid of any true spiritual nourishment whatever. For it is not mere words that nourish the soul, but God Himself, and unless and until the hearers find God in personal experience they are not the better for having heard the truth. The Bible is not an end in itself, but a means to bring men to an intimate and satisfying knowledge of God, that they may enter into Him, that they may delight in His Presence, may taste and know the inner sweetness of the very God Himself in the core and center of their hearts.

"This book is a modest attempt to aid God's hungry children, so to find Him. Nothing here is new except in the sense that it is a discovery which my own heart has made of spiritual realities most delightful and wonderful to me. Others before me have gone much farther into these holy mysteries than I have done, but if my fire is not large it is yet real, and there may be those who can light their candle at its flame."[1]

BELOVED, BEFORE ALL ELSE,

WE MUST LEARN TO WORSHIP GOD!

"Give unto the LORD the glory due unto his name; worship the LORD in the beauty of holiness."

— Psalms 29:2

---

[1] **A.W. Tozer**, <u>The Pursuit of God</u>, from the preface (Chicago, IL) June 16, 1948

THE KEY TO WORSHIP

To many Christians, this doctrine may seem unimportant; few even know what it is. The only thing they may know about a *priest* comes from reading the Old Testament. Some have lived all their lives in a free society where the government had no power to dictate to them how they should worship. Therefore they have no experience living in a nation that has a *state church* setup where only *approved* government churches and pastors are allowed to preach and to conduct worship services. In such oppressed countries, Christians and preachers are arrested and persecuted because they will not conform to the dictates of the powers that be. Furthermore, most Christians know little or nothing about church history. They may not have even heard of the *Dark Ages* when the Roman Catholic Church was the *official* state religion of some European countries and dissenting heretics were tortured to death as infidels. Few American Christians really know anything about living in spiritual bondage under a Roman Catholic *priest* who supposedly acts as the mediator between them and God. Having known only the one true mediator between God and man, the Lord Jesus Christ (I Timothy 2:5), they can little appreciate their great privilege to have **no priest but Christ** over them.

This doctrine of the *priesthood of the believer*, is the belief that each born-again believer has been granted the privilege of direct access to God. It is an *office* to which every believer is appointed.

> **"Therefore being justified by faith, we have peace with God through our Lord Jesus Christ:**
>
> **"By whom also we have access by faith into this grace wherein we stand, and rejoice in hope of the glory of God."**
>
> **— Romans 5:1-2**

There remains then, no need of any *earthly* representative who must intercede *for us* and offer sacrifices *in our behalf*. Our only priest and representative to God is the Lord Jesus Christ Himself.

"The Priesthood Speaks of REPRESENTATION

"It implies the principle of representation. The institution of the office was God's gracious provision for a people at a distance from Him, who needed one to appear in the divine presence in their behalf. The high priest was to act for men in things pertaining to God, "to make propitiation for the sins of the people" (Hebrews 2:17). He was the mediator who ministered for the guilty..."[2]

The Bible says

"For every high priest taken from among men is ORDAINED FOR MEN in things pertaining to God, that he may offer both gifts and sacrifices for sins:

"And no man taketh this honour unto himself, but he that is called of God, as was Aaron.

"So also Christ glorified not himself to be made an high priest; but he that said unto him, Thou art my Son, to day have I begotten thee.

"And being made perfect, he became the author of eternal salvation unto all them that obey him;"

— Hebrews 5:1, 4-5, 9

The Old Testament priests were *"ordained for man"* so that they might represent man before God *"in things pertaining to God."* They served as a mediator, offered the sacrifices and performed all the ceremonial acts of worship. They were keepers of the Tabernacle from the time of Moses to the time of Solomon, and later of the Temple in Jerusalem. They would pray, burn incense and sprinkle the blood of the sacrifices upon the altar. This was a vital ministry to the spiritual needs of the nation until the New Testament was established. Then, everything changed. Now

---

[2] International Standard Bible Encyclopedia

the offering of the blood of the Lord Jesus Christ has opened the way for every believer to have access to God.

> **"How much more shall the blood of CHRIST, who through the eternal Spirit OFFERED HIMSELF without spot to God, purge your conscience from dead works to serve the living God?**
>
> **"And for this cause HE IS THE MEDIATOR of the new testament, that by means of death, for the redemption of the transgressions that were under the first testament, they which are called might receive the promise of eternal inheritance.**
> — **Hebrews 9:14-15**

There are many religions and many priests, but we alone have a high priest who is perfect (Hebrews 5:9). Only *our* high priest could offer *Himself* as a sacrifice, well pleasing unto God, for our redemption (Hebrews 9:14-15). By His obedience unto death, we are made righteous (Romans 5:19). Therefore, *every* believer can go directly to God as a result of our right standing *in Him*. As born-again believers we are now our own priests before a Holy God, not by any merit on our part, but entirely by His grace.

➲ Our chief privilege as believer-priests is **ACCESS TO GOD**

Can you imagine what it was like to live in Old Testament times? There was the tabernacle in the center of the camp of Israel. Inside, the Levite priests would minister unto the Lord. Then, once a year, Aaron (or one of his descendants) would enter into the very presence of God, on the great day of atonement (Exodus 30:10).

> **"Then verily the first covenant had also ordinances of divine service, and a worldly sanctuary.**
>
> **"For there was a tabernacle made; the first, wherein was the candlestick, and the table, and the shewbread; which is called the sanctuary.**
>
> **"And after the second veil, the tabernacle which is called the Holiest of all;**

> "Now when these things were thus ordained, the priests went always into the first tabernacle, accomplishing the SERVICE of God.
>
> "But into the second went the high priest alone ONCE EVERY YEAR, not without blood, which he offered for himself, and for the errors of the people:"
>
> — Hebrews 9:1-3, 6-7

Only the high priest could stand in the presence of God in the *"Holiest of all."* What great fear and wonder Israel must have felt, knowing that God was present among them in the tabernacle, but being forbidden to enter into His presence because of their sin. That earthly tabernacle was built after the pattern of the tabernacle in Heaven (Exodus 25:9). Below is an illustration of the layout of the earthly tabernacle with its three sections.

⮒ The Outer Court

⮒ The Holy Place

⮒ The Most Holy Place (Holy of Holies)

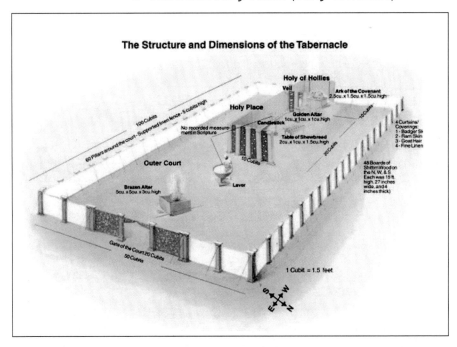

Inside the tabernacle, a vail (curtain) separated the Holy Place from the Outer Court (Exodus 26:31-35). Once inside the Holy Place, another vail separated it from the Most Holy Place. Beyond that second vail, in the Most Holy Place, dwelt the ark of the covenant, and there the priest met with God to sprinkle the blood of the sacrificial lamb on the mercy seat of the Ark of the Covenant.

God spoke out of the midst of the burning bush, warning Moses

> **"Draw not nigh hither... the place whereon thou standest is holy ground"**   **— Exodus 3:5**

Again, when Moses and Aaron went up Mount Sinai to meet God, the people were forbidden to even come near the mount (Exodus 19).

> **"And thou shalt set bounds unto the people round about, saying, Take heed to yourselves, that ye go not up into the mount, or touch the border of it: whosoever toucheth the mount shall be surely put to death:"**
> **— Exodus 19:12**

Later, when the tabernacle was built, only the high priest was allowed to enter the third court of the tabernacle, for there in the holiest place, God communed with man.

> **"And let them make me a sanctuary; that I may dwell among them."**   **— Exodus 25:8**

> **"And there I will meet with thee, and I will commune with thee from above the mercy seat, from between the two cherubims which are upon the ark of the testimony, of all things which I will give thee in commandment unto the children of Israel."**
> **— Exodus 25:22**

But, under the New Testament *every* born again believer is *invited* to *"draw nigh unto God."* As we obey this command, He then draws nigh unto us that we may commune with Him as priests.

> **"For the law made nothing perfect, but the bringing in of a better hope did; by the which we DRAW NIGH unto God."** — Hebrews 7:19

> **"DRAW NIGH to God, and he will draw nigh to you..."** — James 4:8

As born again believers, we are nothing but sinners, saved by grace. Who are we that a king should die for us (Job 7:17; 15:14; Psalm 8:4)? But He *did!* We humans are such frail, insignificant creatures, with no right to even exist, but for the pleasure of the Lord (Revelation 4:11). But, though man is as nothing, we, believers, have a standing invitation to enter into the presence of Almighty God, by prayer, **anytime** we desire. **We have access to Him**!

But, how much value do we place on this wonderful privilege? Have we ever really thought about what it means to have an "audience with God?"

➲ **YOU** (Christian husband, wife, mother, father, young person; whoever you are) are a priest to God.

➲ **YOU** have access to His holy presence anytime you desire, without the need of any human intermediary.

We have only one mediator between us and God, the man, Christ Jesus (I Timothy 2:5), our Great High Priest. Two thousand years ago the veil of the temple was rent (Mark 15:38), the Old Testament priesthood was abolished and our entrance to the holiest was guaranteed by our Saviour's one sacrifice, forever.

In the letter to the Hebrews, we read of the believer's privilege

> **"Having therefore, brethren, boldness to ENTER INTO THE HOLIEST by the blood of Jesus,**

> **"By a new and living way, which he hath consecrated for us, through the veil, that is to say, his flesh;"**
>
> — Hebrews 10:19-20

Andrew Murray gives helpful commentary on these verses.

"Enter Into the Holiest.

"[I]t is a call to all lukewarm, half-hearted Christians, no longer to remain in the outer court of the tabernacle, content with the 'hope' that their sins are pardoned. Nor even to be satisfied with having entered the Holy Place, and there 'doing the service' of the tabernacle, while the veil still hinders the full fellowship with the living God and His love. It calls to enter in through the rent veil, into the place into which the blood has been brought, and where the High Priest lives, there to live and walk and work, always in the presence of the Father. It is a call to all doubting, thirsting believers, who long for a better life than they have yet known, to cast aside their doubts, and to believe that this is what Christ has indeed done and brought within the reach of each one of us: *He has opened the way into the Holiest!...*

"Enter Into the Holiest.

"Oh, the glory of the message. For fifteen centuries Israel had a sanctuary with a 'Holiest of All,' into which, under pain of death, no one might enter. Its one witness was: man cannot dwell in God's presence, cannot abide in His fellowship. And now, how changed is all! As then the warning sounded: *'No admittance! Enter not!'* So now the call goes forth: *'Enter in!'* The veil is rent; the Holiest is open; God waits to welcome you to His bosom. Henceforth you are to live with Him. This is the message of the Epistle: Child! Thy Father longs for thee to enter, to dwell, and to go out no more for ever...

"Enter Into the Holiest.

"[T]he measure of our boldness is the worth God attaches to the **BLOOD** of Jesus....

"Boldness in the **BLOOD** of Jesus.

"Everything depends upon our apprehension of what that means. If the **BLOOD** be to us what it is to God, the boldness which God means it to give will fill our hearts. As we saw in chapter 9, what the **BLOOD** has effected in rending the veil and cleansing the heavens, and giving Jesus, the son of man, access to God, will be the measure of what it will effect within us, making our heart God's sanctuary, and fitting us for perfect fellowship with the Holy One. The more we honor the **BLOOD** in its infinite worth, the more will it prove its mighty energy and efficacy, opening heaven to us and in us, giving us, in divine power, the real living experience of what the entrance into the Holiest is.

"The **BLOOD** of Jesus.

"The life is the **BLOOD**. As the value of this life, so the value of the **BLOOD**. In Christ there was the life of God; infinite as God, is the worth and the power of that **BLOOD**. In Christ, there was the life of man in its perfection; in His humility, and obedience to the Father, and self-sacrifice, that which made Him unspeakably well pleasing to the Father. That **BLOOD** of Jesus (who was both God and man), poured out in a death that was a perfect fulfillment of God's will, and a perfect victory over all the temptations of sin and self, effected an everlasting atonement for sin, and put it forever out of the way, destroying death and him that had the power of it. Therefore it was, that in the **BLOOD** of the everlasting covenant Jesus was raised from the dead; that in His own **BLOOD**, as our Head and Surety, He entered heaven; and that that **BLOOD** is now forever in heaven, in the same place of honor as GOD, THE JUDGE OF ALL, AND JESUS THE MEDIATOR (12:24). It is this **BLOOD**, now in heaven before God for us, that is our boldness to enter in, even into the very Holiest of All.

"Beloved Christian! The **BLOOD** of Jesus! The **BLOOD** of the Lamb! O think what it means. God gave it for your redemption. God accepted it when His Son entered heaven and presented it on your behalf. God has it forever in His sight as the fruit, the infinitely well-pleasing proof, of His Son's obedience unto death. God points you to it, and asks you to believe in the divine satisfaction it gives to Him, in its omnipotent energy, in its everlasting sufficiency. Oh, will you not this day believe that that

BLOOD gives you, sinful and feeble as you are, liberty, confidence, boldness to draw nigh, to enter the very Holiest? Yes, believe it, that the **BLOOD**, and the **BLOOD** alone, but the **BLOOD** most surely, brings you into the very presence, into the living and abiding fellowship, of the everlasting God. And let your response to God's message concerning the **BLOOD**, and the boldness it gives you, be nothing less than this, that this very moment you go with the utmost confidence, and take your place in the most intimate fellowship with God. And if your heart condemn you, or coldness or unbelief appear to make a real entrance impossible, rest not till you believe and prove to the full, the power of the **BLOOD** in very deed to bring you nigh. HAVING BOLDNESS BY THE BLOOD OF JESUS, LET US DRAW NEAR!"[3]

The Old Testament priest was a man ordained by God, to serve in the office ordained by God; a man called of God, to minister to God.

> **"And thou shalt speak unto all that are wise hearted, whom I have filled with the spirit of wisdom, that they may make Aaron's garments to consecrate him, that he may minister unto me in the priest's office."   — Exodus 28:3**

> **"For every high priest taken from among men is ORDAINED for men in things pertaining to God, that he may offer both gifts and sacrifices for sins:**
> **"And no man taketh this honour unto himself, but he that is CALLED OF GOD, as was Aaron."**
>
> **— Hebrews 5:1, 4**

An Old Testament priest's primary function was to prepare an altar where he would meet God. There he would worship and minister unto the Lord through sacrifices.

---

[3] **Andrew Murray**, The Holiest of All — A Devotional Exposition of the Epistle to the Hebrews, chapter 10, vss. 19-25.

> **"But the LORD, who brought you up out of the land of Egypt with great power and a stretched out arm, him shall ye fear, and him shall ye WORSHIP, and to him shall ye do SACRIFICE."**   **— II Kings 17:36**

Notice that WORSHIP comes before SACRIFICE. Furthermore, there is no true "sacrifice" unto God without "obedience" to God.

> **"And Samuel said, Hath the LORD as great delight in burnt offerings and sacrifices, as in obeying the voice of the LORD? Behold, TO OBEY IS BETTER THAN SACRIFICE, and to hearken than the fat of rams."**   **— I Samuel 15:22**

➲ The word "priest" is first used in Genesis 14:18.

> **"And Melchizedek king of Salem brought forth bread and wine: and he was the priest of the most high God."**   **— Genesis 14:18**

Interestingly, Melchizedek presented only the *memorials* of sacrifice, bread and wine. Even so, the Lord Jesus Christ (a priest after the order of Melchizedek) presented to the apostles, bread and wine for **a memorial**[4] of His great sacrifice.

➲ The first sacrifice in the Bible (Genesis 3:21), was made by God, Himself.

> **"Unto Adam also and to his wife did the LORD God make coats of skins, and clothed them."**
> **— Genesis 3:21**

As Adam and Eve were about to be expelled from the beautiful garden that God had prepared for them, they knew that the intimate fellowship they enjoyed together with Him was about to end.

---

[4] **memorial** — Something that serves to honor or keep alive a memory: memorial, commemoration, keepsake, memento, monument, relic, **remembrance**, shrine, souvenir, **token**. American Heritage Dictionary

No longer would they hear *"the voice of the LORD God walking in the garden in the cool of the day"* (Genesis 3:8). Now, Adam and Eve realized they were naked, and they were ashamed. Then, they *"sewed fig leaves together, and made themselves aprons"* (Genesis 3:7). But it was a poor substitute for the innocency they had previously enjoyed. So, God Himself, in one last act of Fatherly love before they left the sanctuary and fellowship of the garden, made coats of skins to cover the nakedness of Adam and Eve. But, in order to obtain the skins, it was necessary that an innocent animal die. As we understand the typology of the lamb throughout the Bible, it is clear that the *"coats of skins"* were lamb skins (cf. Genesis 4:4, 22:8; Exodus 12). So, Adam and Eve were witness to the first blood shed upon the earth, a direct consequence of their sin.

➲ Abel was the first man to offer a blood sacrifice unto the Lord. As believers do today, Abel acted as his own priest.

> **"And in process of time it came to pass, that Cain brought of the fruit of the ground an offering unto the LORD.**
> **"And Abel, he also brought of the firstlings of his flock and of the fat thereof. And the LORD had respect unto Abel and to his offering:"**
> **— Genesis 4:3-4**

We may assume that God had *'respect'* unto Abel's offering because it was the right offering; the offering that God required.

> **"By faith Abel offered unto God a more excellent sacrifice than Cain, by which he obtained witness that he was righteous, God testifying of his gifts: and by it he being dead yet speaketh."**   **— Hebrews 11:4**

No doubt the story of the sacrifice of the lamb that God provided was passed on to their children. Both Cain and Abel knew what sacrifice was acceptable; only the blood of the lamb.

➲ In fulfillment of the typology begun in Genesis, it was God who made the **final sacrifice** as well— offering Himself as a ransom for our sin at Calvary. Once again, God provided Himself a lamb just as He did for Abraham. But for this final sacrifice, the lamb He provided was Himself.

> **"And walk in love, as Christ also hath loved us, and hath given HIMSELF for us an offering and A SACRIFICE to God for a sweetsmelling savour."**
> — **Ephesians 5:2**

> **"For then must he often have suffered since the foundation of the world: but now once in the end of the world hath he appeared to put away sin by the sacrifice of himself."** — **Hebrews 9:26**

Today, there remains only ONE offering for sin that is acceptable to God. That sacrifice was made 2000 years ago when the Lamb of God "put away sin by the sacrifice of himself." The Catholic church's *continual* *"sacrifice* of the mass" is an abomination to God. There is no longer any priest authorized to make a literal sacrifice unto God, nor is there any ongoing sacrifice for sin that is acceptable to Him.

PREPARING AN ALTAR

The Old Testament Altar

As we continue through the book of Genesis, we see that the building of altars and the offering of sacrifices are found throughout. An altar was simply a place to meet God. But the purpose of that meeting was always **to present a sacrifice unto the Lord.**

Noah built an altar[5]

> **"And NOAH builded an ALTAR unto the LORD; and took of every clean beast, and of every clean fowl, and offered burnt offerings on the ALTAR."**
> **— Genesis 8:20**

God had purged the whole earth of all mankind, except for the eight men and women who are in the ark, and part of one righteous man's household. Naturally, the first thing in Noah's mind, after landing safely in this new world, was to offer a sacrifice unto the God, Who saved him. He was acting as a priest to his family.

Abraham built altars

> **"And the LORD appeared unto Abram and said, Unto thy seed will I give this land: and there builded he an ALTAR unto the LORD, who appeared unto him."**
> **"And he removed from thence unto a mountain on the east of Bethel, and pitched his tent, having Bethel on the west, and Hai on the east: and there he builded an ALTAR unto the LORD, and called upon the name of the LORD.**
> **— Genesis 12:7-8**

---

[5] The word "altar" occurs in the Bible for the first time in Genesis 8:20. Obviously it is not the first altar ever built, but this is the first time the word "altar" is used.

In Genesis 12:6-8 we find the first mention of an altar since Noah (Genesis 8:20), showing that building altars and making sacrifices continued.

> "Then Abram removed his tent, and came and dwelt in the plain of Mamre, which is in Hebron, and built there an ALTAR unto the LORD."
> — Genesis 13:18

> "And they came to the place which God had told him of; and Abraham built an ALTAR there, and laid the wood in order, and bound Isaac his son, and laid him on the ALTAR upon the wood."   — Genesis 22:9

Isaac built an altar

> "And he builded an ALTAR there, and called upon the name of the LORD, and pitched his tent there: and there Isaac's servants digged a well." — Genesis 26:25

Jacob built an altar

> "And he erected there an ALTAR, and called it Elelohe-Israel."   — Genesis 33:20

Moses built an altar

> "And Moses built an ALTAR, and called the name of it Jehovahnissi:"   — Exodus 17:15

In the tabernacle (and later in the temple) two altars were built.

> "(1.) The ALTAR OF BURNT OFFERING (Exodus 30:28), called also the "BRASEN ALTAR" (Exodus 39:39) and "the table of the Lord" (Malachi 1:7)...

> "This altar, as erected in the tabernacle, is described in Exodus 27:1-8...

> "In Solomon's temple the altar was of larger dimensions (II Chronicles 4:1; cf. I Kings 8:22, 64; 9:25), and was made wholly of brass, covering a structure of stone or earth. This altar was renewed by Asa (II Chronicles 15:8). It was removed by Ahaz (II Kings 16:14), and "cleansed"

by Hezekiah, in the latter part of whose reign it was rebuilt. It was finally broken up and carried away by the Babylonians (Jeremiah 52:17).

"After the return from captivity it was re-erected (Ezra 3:3,6) on the same place where it had formerly stood... When Antiochus Epiphanes pillaged Jerusalem the altar of burnt offering was taken away.

"Again the altar was erected by Herod, and remained in its place till the destruction of Jerusalem by the Romans (70 AD).

"(2.) The ALTAR OF INCENSE (Exodus 30:1-10), called also 'THE GOLDEN ALTAR' (Exodus 39:38; Numbers 4:11), stood in the holy place 'before the vail that is by the ark of the testimony.' On this altar sweet spices were continually burned with fire taken from the brazen altar. The morning and the evening services were commenced by the high priest offering incense on this altar. The burning of the incense was a type of prayer (Psalm 141:2; Revelation 5:8; 8:3-4)."[6]

The New Testament Altar

In the book of Hebrews, new truth is revealed about another altar.

> **"We have an ALTAR, whereof they have no right to eat which serve the tabernacle."**   **— Hebrews 13:10**

Here, the word "altar" does not refer to the cross upon which Christ was crucified. Neither does it speak of the Lord's table, whereupon the representative elements of His flesh and blood are presented to the church at the Lord's Supper. This altar is Christ himself; He is altar, sacrifice, and priest.

---

[6] **Matthew George Easton**, Easton's Bible Dictionary, (Thomas Nelson) 1897. Easton was a Scottish Presbyterian minister.

"For then must he often have suffered since the foundation of the world: but now ONCE in the end of the world hath he appeared to put away sin by the sacrifice of himself."   **— Hebrews 9:26**

J.C. Ryle reminds us of this

"If any one believes that Paul's words to the Hebrews, 'We have an altar' (Hebrews 13:10), are a proof that the Lord's table is an altar, I remind him 'Christians have an altar where they partake. That altar is Christ our Lord, who is Altar, Priest, and Sacrifice, all in One.'"[7]

A.W. Pink adds

"In view of its significance, its importance, its hallowed associations, one can readily imagine what it meant to a converted Jew to abandon the altar of Judaism. Unto his unbelieving brethren he would necessarily appear as a renegade of his fathers, an apostate from God, and a fool to himself. Their taunt would be, In turning your back upon Judaism you have lost everything: you have *no altar!* Why, you are worse off than the wretched Samaritans, for they *do* have a place and system of worship on mount Gerizim: whereas you Christians have *nothing!* But here the apostle turns the tables upon them: he affirms that not only do we '*have* an altar,' but it was one which those who still identified themselves with the temple and its services had no right to. In turning from Judaism to Christ the believing Hebrew had left the shadow for the substance, the figure for the reality; whereas those who despised and rejected Christ merely had that which was become 'weak and beggarly elements' (Galatians 4:9).

"The sad failure of the great mass of the Jews, under the Gospel-preaching of the apostles, to turn their affections unto things above, where Christ had passed within the veil, and their stubbornness in clinging to the tangible system at Jerusalem, was something more than a peculiarity of that nation— it exemplified the universal fondness of man for that which is *material* in religion, and his

---

[7] **J.C. Ryle,** The Lord's Supper 1816-1900 (modernized version by Tony Capoccia.)

disrelish of that which is strictly *spiritual*. In Judaism there was much that was addressed to the sense, herein too lies the power and secret of Rome's success: the strength of its appeal to the natural man lies in its sensuous show. Though Christians have no visible manifestation of the Divine glory on earth to which they may draw near when they worship, they do have access to the Throne of Grace in Heaven; but it is only the truly regenerate who prefer the substance to the shadow.

"'We have an altar.' Our altar, unlike that of Judaism, is inside the veil: 'whither the Forerunner is for us entered, even Jesus' (Hebrews 6:20), after that He had appeared here upon earth to put away sin by the sacrifice of Himself. To the Christian comes the blessed exhortation,

> **'Having therefore, brethren, boldness to enter into the Holiest by the blood of Jesus,**
>
> **'By a new and living way, which He hath consecrated for us, through the veil, that is to say, His flesh;**
>
> **'And having a High Priest, over the house of God,**
>
> **'Let us draw near with a true heart in full assurance of faith.**
>
> **— Hebrews 10:19-22'**

"'We have an altar,' namely, Christ, and He is the ONLY altar which *God owns,* and the ONLY one which must be recognized by us. For almost nineteen centuries — since God employed the Romans to destroy Jerusalem— the Jews have been without an altar, and are so to this day. For Romanists[8] to *invent* an altar, and make it both the foundation and center of their entire idolatrous system, is the height of presumption, and a fearful insult to Christ and the sufficiency of His sacrifice. If those 'which serve the tabernacle'— they who continued officiating at Jerusalem in the days when the apostle wrote this epistle— had 'no right' to 'eat' of the Christian's altar, that is, enjoy and derive benefit from the person and sacrifice of Christ, then, how much less have the pope and his satellites [9]

---

[8] Roman Catholics

[9] **satellite** — 5. A nation dominated politically and economically by another

any title to the benefits of Christ while they so wickedly usurp His place and prerogative..." [10]

And what is this 'idolatrous system'? Here is the official teaching of the Roman Catholic Church regarding THEIR altar and sacrifice, taken from *The What and Why of Catholicism* (with the Imprimatur [11] of the late Roman Catholic Cardinal, Joseph Spellman):

> "The Sacrifice of the Mass forms a pivot upon which all else turns. If it is what Catholics believe it is, then here is the greatest external manifestation of the love of God for man and the most magnificent testimonial to the validity of Catholicism; but if it be false, it is the worse farce and blasphemy ever perpetrated upon God or man, and the Catholic faith collapses into nothingness." [12]

Cardinal Spellman realized the significance of the altar and sacrifice, and gave an accurate assessment of its prominence in Roman Catholic theology. He knew the two alternatives, but he made the wrong choice. The sacrifice of the mass is indeed "the worse farce and blasphemy ever perpetrated upon God or man."

Furthermore, we read in *St. Peter's Catechism*,

> "The Mass is a REAL SACRIFICE because in it a Victim is OFFERED BY A PRIEST for the purpose of reconciling man with God." [13]

The 'sacrifice of the Mass' does not 'reconcile' anyone with God! Reconciliation is made only by the blood of the cross (II Corinthians 5:17-19; Ephesians 2:16; Colossians 1:20), and there is no need to repeat it— for, in Christ's own words, "it is

---

nation. American Heritage Dictionary

[10] **A.W. Pink**, An Exposition of Hebrews, (Baker Books)

[11] Official seal of the Roman Catholic Church denoting material that is "approved reading for Catholics."

[12] **Francis Joseph Spellman** (1889-1967) What and Why of Catholicism, (Joseph F. Wagner, New York 1961) Imprimatur and nihil obstat. Spellman was appointed archbishop of Archdiocese of New York diocese in 1939 and cardinal in 1946.

[13] St. Peter's Catechism, (1972), p. 48

finished." As the gospel song says "[T]hey will never crucify Him again," for He is risen (Matthew 20:19; Hebrews 6:6).

From the *Catholic Catechism*, John Hardon (1975):

> "The sacrifice on the altar is no mere 'commemoration' of Calvary, but A TRUE AND PROPER ACT OF SACRIFICE whereby Christ, the high priest, by an unbloody immolation (sacrifice) offers himself a most acceptable victim to the eternal father, AS HE DID ON THE CROSS."[14]

Never forget— it was the **Roman government** who crucified the Lord Jesus Christ two thousand years ago, and it is the **Roman church** that claims to sacrifice Him continually today (Hebrews 6:6); it is the church of the Antichrist, described in Revelation 17:3-9.

We cannot emphasize enough, the importance of Hebrews 9:26 and 13:10. Even as **"their rock"** is not **"our Rock"** (Deuteronomy 32:31) and **"their gospel"** not **"our gospel"** (II Corinthians 11:4; Galatians 1:6-7), neither is **"their altar,"** **"our altar"** (Hebrews 13:10).

Throughout the Bible, altars were always elevated (lifted up), so as to be conspicuously exalted.[15,16] Therefore, our Savior had to be "lifted up" and sacrificed on a cruel, rough and bloody altar.

> **"And as Moses lifted up the serpent in the wilderness, even so must the Son of man be LIFTED UP:"**
> — John 3:14

> **"Then said Jesus unto them, When ye have LIFTED UP the Son of man, then shall ye know that I am he, and that I do nothing of myself; but as my Father hath taught me, I speak these things."**   — John 8:28

---

[14] **John Hardon,** The Catholic Catechism, (Random House, Inc. 1975) nihil obstat & imprimatur.

[15] **altar** — noun 1. An elevated place or structure before which religious ceremonies may be enacted or upon which sacrifices may be offered. The American Heritage Dictionary

[16] Strong's Exhaustive Concordance, reference 5312. υθοω **hupsoo** hoop-so'-o from 5311; to elevate (literally or figuratively):— exalt, lift up (cf. Greek 5311).

> "And I, if I be LIFTED UP from the earth, will draw
> all men unto me."   — John 12:32

The Passover supper had been **a memorial** to the sacrifice of the Passover lamb whose shed blood, applied to each household, stayed the judgment of God.

> "And the blood shall be to you for a TOKEN upon
> the houses where ye are: and when I see the blood, I
> will pass over you, and the plague shall not be upon
> you to destroy you, when I smite the land of Egypt.
>
> "And this day shall be unto you for a MEMORIAL;
> and ye shall keep it a feast to the LORD throughout
> your generations; ye shall keep it a feast by AN ORDI-
> NANCE for ever."
>   — Exodus 12:13-14

In like manner, our Lord instituted **a memorial** to "the Lamb of God which taketh away the sin of the world" (John 1:29). It was to be a "remembrance" of His great "sacrifice for sins" (Hebrews 10:12). We commonly refer to it as "the Lord's supper." By it we are to remember Him and His death. This "memorial" is "in remembrance of" His death.

> "For I have received of the Lord that which also I
> delivered unto you, That the Lord Jesus the same
> night in which he was betrayed took bread:
>
> "And when he had given thanks, he brake it, and
> said, Take, eat: this is my body, which is broken for
> you: this do in REMEMBRANCE of me.
>
> "After the same manner also he took the cup, when
> he had supped, saying, This cup is the new testament
> in my blood: this do ye, as oft as ye drink it, in
> REMEMBRANCE of me.
>
> "For as often as ye eat this bread, and drink this
> cup, ye do shew THE LORD'S DEATH till he come."
>
>   — I Corinthians 11:23-26

"[T]he Lord of glory" (I Corinthians 2:8) agonized on the Mount of Olives as He prayed;

> **"Saying, Father, if thou be willing, remove this cup from me: nevertheless not my will, but thine, be done."**   **— Luke 22:42**

He despised the shame of that cruel cross of Calvary (Luke 23:33), but He endured it all because of "the joy that was set before him."

> **"Looking unto Jesus the author and finisher of our faith; who for THE JOY THAT WAS SET BEFORE HIM endured the cross, DESPISING THE SHAME, and is set down at the right hand of the throne of God."**
> **— Hebrews 12:2**

What was the "*JOY that was set before Him*"?

- ➲ The **JOY** of pleasing the Father (John 8:29; II Peter 1:17)

- ➲ The **JOY** of victory over Satan and death (Hebrews 2:14; Revelation 20:1-10, 14; 21:4)

- ➲ The **JOY** of judgment against sin (Proverbs 21:15)

- ➲ The **JOY** of receiving His kingdom (Luke 10:21-22)

- ➲ The **JOY** of redeeming the lost (Matthew 18:11)

- ➲ The **JOY** of demonstrating His love (John 3:16; Romans 8:39)

- ➲ The **JOY** of purchasing His bride and preparing a place for her in eternity (Isaiah 62:5; Revelation 19:7; 21:9)

Paul exhorted the believers at Ephesus

> **"Be ye therefore followers of God, as dear children;**
>
> **"And walk in love, as Christ also hath loved us, and hath given himself for us an offering and A SACRIFICE to God for A SWEETSMELLING SAVOUR."**
>
> **— Ephesians 5:1-2**

Because of His great love for us, He "hath given himself for us." What a joyous meal is "the Lord's supper," and what a privilege is granted to those who are redeemed by the blood of the Lamb, that we might partake of it. It is shameful how little emphasis is set upon this ordinance in most Baptist churches today, especially since it was established by the Lord Himself. Israel kept the Passover for thousands of years, and does so till this very day. Should we not also be faithful to observe the greatest event of human history, or eternity, the sacrifice of the Lamb of God for the sins of the world?

> **"That ye shall say, It is the SACRIFICE of the LORD'S passover, who passed over the houses of the children of Israel in Egypt, when he smote the Egyptians, and delivered our houses. And the people bowed the head and worshipped."   — Exodus 12:27**

That passover is a reminder to Israel of their deliverance from the bondage of Egypt. We have infinitely more to be thankful for and are even *commanded* to observe the Lord's supper, but rarely do it. It is to "shew the Lord's death till he come." Yet, many Christians put tremendous emphasis on the remembrance of His *birth*, which the Lord never mentioned at all, while putting so little emphasis on his *death*. Something is wrong. Is it not obvious that we put emphasis on that which is most pleasing to the flesh, rather than the spirit?

Israel was *commanded* to REMEMBER the "sacrifice of the Lord's passover" by which THEY were delivered. As born again believers, we are *commanded* to REMEMBER the sacrifice of the Lord's Passover by which WE were delivered.

The believer's only approach to God is by the ONE ALTAR of the sacrifice of the Lamb of God on Mount Calvary two thousand years ago. There, God and man were reconciled (Romans 5).

> **"For if, when we were enemies, we were RECON-CILED to God by the death of his Son, much more, being reconciled, we shall be saved by his life."**
>
> **— Romans 5:10**

> **"For there is one God, and ONE MEDIATOR between God and men, the man Christ Jesus;"**
>
> **— I Timothy 2:5**

> **"Jesus saith unto him, I am the way, the truth, and the life: no man cometh unto the Father, but by me."**
>
> **— John 14:6**

> **"Neither is there salvation in any other: for there is NONE OTHER NAME under heaven given among men, whereby we must be saved."   — Acts 4:12**

There is no other mediator, neither could there be another. Therefore, the "virgin Mary" cannot be a mediator, nor can *any* Roman Catholic priest who ever lived.

➲ Only in the person of Christ, was God manifest in the flesh.

> **"And without controversy great is the mystery of godliness: God was manifest in the flesh, justified in the Spirit, seen of angels, preached unto the Gentiles, believed on in the world, received up into glory."**
>
> **— I Timothy 3:16**

> **"But this man, after he had offered one sacrifice for sins for ever, sat down on the right hand of God;"**
>
> **— Hebrews 10:12**

Now, He has made every believer to be their own priest on Earth. Therefore, we have no other mediator upon this earth.

"And from Jesus Christ, who is the faithful witness, and the first begotten of the dead, and the prince of the kings of the earth. Unto him that loved us, and washed us from our sins in his own blood,

"And hath made us kings and PRIESTS UNTO GOD and his Father; to him be glory and dominion for ever and ever. Amen."

— Revelation 1:5-6

➲ He is our **altar**
(the Lord's Supper is a memorial in remembrance)

➲ He is our **sacrifice**, made once forever
(therefore we are to give *our* bodies, a living sacrifice)

➲ He is our **High Priest**
(and he has made us "priests and kings" unto Him)

We certainly can offer no other sacrifice for our sins, but we are to offer spiritual sacrifices as a sweetsmelling savour unto the Lord.

MINISTERING UNTO THE LORD

The priest of the Old Testament was to minister unto the Lord. Even so, the born again believer today is to minister unto the Lord. What does it mean, "to minister"? It simply means to serve Him.

The American Heritage Dictionary says [17]

➲ **min-is-ter,** v. intr. **1.** To attend to the wants and needs of another:

➲ **serve,** v. tr. **1.** To work for. To be a servant to. **5.** To be of assistance to or promote the interests of; to aid.

We see this plainly, in the following scriptures.

"From thirty years old and upward even unto fifty years old, every one that came to do the SERVICE of the MINISTRY, and the SERVICE of the burden in the tabernacle of the congregation,"   — Numbers 4:47

"Then he called his SERVANT that MINISTERED unto him, and said, Put now this woman out from me, and bolt the door after her."   — II Samuel 13:17

"My sons, be not now negligent: for the LORD hath chosen you to stand before him, to SERVE him, and that ye should MINISTER unto him, and burn incense."   — II Chronicles 29:11

"But Jesus called them to him, and saith unto them, Ye know that they which are accounted to rule over the Gentiles exercise lordship over them; and their great ones exercise authority upon them.

"But so shall it not be among you: but whosoever will be great among you, shall be your MINISTER:

"And whosoever of you will be the chiefest, shall be SERVANT of all.

— Mark 10:42-44

Priests are to minister; that is clear. And the ministry of Israel's priests was laid out in great detail in the Old Testament. They were to attend the tabernacle, offer sacrifices and worship the Lord.

Old Testament Ministry

Israel's priests ministered unto the Lord

"And take thou unto thee Aaron thy brother, and his sons with him, from among the children of Israel, that he may MINISTER unto me in the priest's office, even Aaron, Nadab and Abihu, Eleazar and Ithamar, Aaron's sons."   — Exodus 28:1

"And the sons of Aaron the priest shall put fire upon the altar, and lay the wood in order upon the fire:"   — Leviticus 1:7

"And the fire upon the altar shall be burning in it; it shall not be put out: and the priest shall burn wood on it every morning, and lay the burnt offering in order upon it; and he shall burn thereon the fat of the peace offerings."   — Leviticus 6:12

And they minister unto the congregation, as well.

"And that ye may teach the children of Israel all the statutes which the LORD hath spoken unto them by the hand of Moses."   — Leviticus 10:11

"Seemeth it but a small thing unto you, that the God of Israel hath separated you from the congregation of Israel, to bring you near to himself to do the SERVICE of the tabernacle of the LORD, and to stand before the congregation to MINISTER unto them?"
— Numbers 16:9

"For the priest's lips should keep knowledge, and they should seek the law at his mouth: for he is the messenger of the LORD of hosts."   — Malachi 2:7

New Testament Ministry

As New Testament believer-priests, we, too, are to minister unto the Lord. Think for a moment; do you see yourself as having ministered unto the Lord throughout this past week, as a priest unto God? And yet that is our wonderful privilege, and our awesome responsibility. There is so much more to being a real Christian than attending meetings, observing ceremonies and keeping certain rules of conduct. If we would take our proper place as a priest unto God, our whole life would be different. But, never forget, we are always to remain a member of a local church and under the authority of a local pastor. This is not a conflict, since the pastor does not intervene in our personal priesthood relationship with God, but only encourages and equips us to carry out our ministry unto the Lord.

As the Old Testament priests ministered unto those in the congregation, so do we, but NO LONGER AS PRIESTS. We now minister to them by the offices of the local church and by the gifts of the Holy Spirit. Furthermore, to the unsaved, we have been given the *"ministry of reconciliation"* by which we are become AMBASSADORS OF CHRIST that they might be *"reconciled to God"* (II Corinthians 5:18-20).

Oh, praise His wonderful name for all that we have become IN HIM. How blessed to have a personal divine relationship with

Almighty God. Yet, He not only allows us to be a lowly servant, but wonder of wonders, ambassadors and priests before men and angels. And what shall it be, in that day, when our Lord cometh for His own? *"Holy, holy, holy, Lord God Almighty, which was, and is, and is to come."* (Revelation 4:8)

Our priestly relationship is only between ourselves as individuals and our God. Our ministry to others can only be by the gifts and power of the Holy Spirit that dwells within every believer (Romans 12). Otherwise, we would be ministering only by the power of the flesh, and that can never bring about the transforming and lasting results that we expect from the working of His power, neither will it effectively magnify His word and His name.

Christ is our great example

"Even as the Son of man came not to be MINIS-TERED unto, but to MINISTER, and to give his life a ransom for many." — Matthew 20:28

As we have done unto others, we have done unto Him

"And the King shall answer and say unto them, Verily I say unto you, Inasmuch as ye have done it unto one of the least of these my brethren, ye have done it unto me." — Matthew 25:40

Those who minister unto the Lord receive direction from Him

"As they MINISTERED to the Lord, and fasted, the Holy Ghost said, Separate me Barnabas and Saul for the work whereunto I have called them." — Acts 13:2

We are to minister sacrificially, consecratedly and according to God's will

"How that in a GREAT TRIAL OF AFFLICTION the abundance of their joy and their DEEP POVERTY abounded unto the riches of their liberality.

"For to their power, I bear record, yea, and BEYOND THEIR POWER they were willing of themselves;

"Praying us with much intreaty that we would receive the gift, and take upon us the fellowship of the MINISTERING to the saints.

"And this they did, not as we hoped, but first GAVE THEIR OWN SELVES to the Lord, and unto us BY THE WILL OF GOD.

— II Corinthians 8:2-5

"For as touching the MINISTERING to the saints, it is superfluous for me to write to you:

— II Corinthians 9:1

We will reap of our ministry what we sow to our ministry

"But this I say, He which soweth sparingly shall reap also sparingly; and he which soweth bountifully shall reap also bountifully."   — II Corinthians 9:6

Dr. Peter S. Ruckman says

"This is a great passage which gives the New Testament standard on *giving*. I would definitely memorize verses 6-8. Verse 6 is known as the 'Law of the Harvest.' You should compare verse 6 with Galatians 6:7-9. The complete law states this:

1. You reap WHAT you sow (Galatians 6:7-8. If you sow to the corrupt flesh, you 'REAP CORRUPTION;' if you sow to the Holy Spirit, the Spirit of life, you 'REAP LIFE EVERLASTING.'

2. You always reap MORE than you sow (John 12:24).

3. You reap according to HOW you sow (II Corinthians 9:6).

➲ If you only sow a little, you will reap a SMALL HARVEST;

➲ If you sow a lot, you will reap a BIG HARVEST.

4. You WILL reap (Galatians 6:9). It may not
be down here. You may not see a harvest
until the Judgment Seat of Christ. But
YOU WILL REAP." [18]

The benefactor never comes up short

"Now he that MINISTERETH seed to the sower
both MINISTER bread for your food, and multiply your
seed sown, and increase the fruits of your righteousness;)"   — II Corinthians 9:10

As glorious and wonderful as it sounds, it is for His glory alone and when we have done all, we have only done our duty.

"I beseech you therefore, brethren, by the mercies
of God, that ye present your bodies a living sacrifice,
holy, acceptable unto God, which is your REASON-
ABLE SERVICE."   — Romans 12:1

"So likewise ye, when ye shall have done all those
things which are commanded you, say, We are
unprofitable servants: we have done that which was
OUR DUTY to do."   — Luke 17:10

"But unto them which are called, both Jews and
Greeks, Christ the power of God, and the wisdom of
God.

"Because the foolishness of God is wiser than
men; and the weakness of God is stronger than men.

"For ye see your calling, brethren, how that not
many wise men after the flesh, not many mighty, not
many noble, are called:

"But God hath chosen the FOOLISH THINGS of the
world to confound the wise; and God hath chosen the
WEAK THINGS of the world to confound the things
which are mighty;

---

[18] **Peter S. Ruckman,** The Books of First and Second Corinthians, The Bible
Believer's Commentary Series; (Bible Baptist Bookstore, Pensacola, FL)

"And BASE THINGS of the world, and THINGS WHICH ARE DESPISED, hath God chosen, yea, and THINGS WHICH ARE NOT, to bring to nought things that are:

"That no flesh should glory in his presence.

"But of him are ye in Christ Jesus, who of God is made unto us wisdom, and righteousness, and sanctification, and redemption:

"That, according as it is written, He that glorieth, let him glory in the Lord."

— I Corinthians 1:24-31

WORSHIPPING THE LORD

I have no doubt that we, Baptists, have heard the best preaching in the world— that is one of our strong points, and we have others. However, worship is something we need to learn more about. Let's take a look at the problems, purpose and preparation in worship.

Problems In Worship

"In 1961, A.W. Tozer[19] gave three messages to the pastors of the Associated Gospel Churches of Canada. His topic was *'Worship: The Missing Jewel of the Evangelical Church.'* In true prophetic fashion, he called for a return to astonishment and wonder at the majesty of God. Then he added:

> 'The God of the modern evangelical rarely astonishes anybody. He manages to stay pretty much within the constitution... very well-behaved, very denominational and very much one of us.'

"In modern evangelicalism, contended Tozer, we work, we have our agendas— in fact, we have almost everything except the spirit of true worship. He defined worship as a humbling but delightful sense of admiring awe, astonished wonder and overpowering love in the presence of the unspeakable Majesty. He reminded the pastors,

> 'We're here to be worshippers first and workers only second... Out of enraptured, admiring, adoring souls God does His work. The work done by a worshipper will have eternity in it.'

---

[19] **Aiden Wilson Tozer (1897-1963),** beloved *Christian & Missionary Alliance* pastor, and author of over forty books that every believer in pursuit of God should read.

"Tozer believed that worship rises and falls with OUR CONCEPT OF GOD and that if there was one terrible disease in the modern church, it was that we do not see God as great as He is:

> 'We're too familiar with God. [T]hat is why I do not believe in these half-converted cowboys who call God, *the Man Upstairs.*'"

"In the Preface to The Knowledge of the Holy, his last book, Tozer stated how important our view of God is:

> 'The church has surrendered her once lofty concept of God and has substituted for it one so low, so ignoble as to be utterly unworthy of thinking, worshipping men. [A] whole new philosophy of the Christian life has resulted from this one basic error.'"[20]

In a similar vein Chuck Swindoll said about worship

"What, then, is worship? Dr. Ron Allen... writes,

> *'Worship is an active response to God whereby we declare His worth.*
>
> 'The English word 'worship' is wonderfully expressive of the act that it describes. This term comes from the Anglo-Saxon *'weorthscipe,'* which then was modified to *'worthship,'* and finally to *'worship.'* Worship means 'to attribute worth' to something or someone.'

"Let me ask you: do you worship where you go to church? 'Yes,' you say, 'I just love the Bible teaching at our church.' That's not my question. 'Oh, yes, the singing is wonderful.' That's not my question either. I know you love the Bible... And you probably love to sing. I'm not asking about those things. I'm asking, do you worship? In the words of John Wesley, the beloved pastor and evangelist, are you *'lost in wonder, love, and praise'* in the midst of your gatherings?

"We are often so caught up in our activities that we tend to:

- worship our work,

- work at our play,

- and play at our worship."[21]

Here are some other meaningful quotes on worship

Robert Coleman

"True worship can only take place when we agree to God sitting, not only on His throne in the center of the universe, but, on the throne that stands in the center of our heart."

Kelly Sparks

"God is not moved or impressed with our worship until our hearts are moved and impressed by Him."

Robert E. Webber

"For years, the church has emphasized evangelism, teaching, fellowship, missions, and service to society to the neglect of the very source of its power— worship."

Baker's Dictionary of Theology

"Worship is pure adoration, the lifting up of the redeemed spirit toward God in contemplation of His holy perfection."[22]

Jerry Solomon

"First, the SPIRIT of worship is important. We are to render 'such homage to God that the entire heart enters into the act.' Whether we are in a time of private praise and adoration, or gathered with the church in corporate proclamation, we are to respond to who God is from the SPIRIT, from the whole of our innermost being.

---

[21] **Chuck Swindoll**, "Discovering the Missing Jewel of Worship," audiocassette series, *Making New Discoveries* (Anaheim, CA, (Insight for Living, 1993), MND2B.

[22] Baker's Dictionary of Theology, p. 561.

"<u>Second</u>, we are to do 'this in full harmony with the TRUTH of God as revealed in his Word.' The concept of responding to God in SPIRIT can give rise to confusing individual expressions if those expressions are not guided by Scripture.

"There must be balance between SPIRIT and TRUTH. One without the other is not complete. 'As some see it, a humble, spiritual attitude means little. According to others, truth or doctrinal soundness is of no importance. Both are one-sided, unbalanced, and therefore wrong. Genuine worshippers worship in SPIRIT and TRUTH.'"[23]

In his book on worship, A.P. Gibbs writes [24]

"We have before indicated that worship has, as one of its basic requirements, the element of wonder. He who ceases to wonder, ceases to worship. The hymn writer has put it thus:

'I stand amazed in the presence
Of Jesus the Nazarene,
And wonder how He could love me,
A sinner, condemned, unclean!

O how wonderful! O how marvelous!
And my song shall ever be,
O how wonderful! Oh how marvelous!
Is my Savior's love to me!'"

While a member of Shady Acres Baptist Church, Houston, Texas (1983), I heard pastor Jack Wood preach a sermon I will never forget; *Have You Lost the Wonder?* Indeed, I had! I was so busy in the work of the ministry that I had lost the wonder and amazement of the God I served. I had begun to fit Him into my

---

[23] **Jerry Solomon** was formerly the Field Director for Probe Ministries. He also served as Associate Pastor at Dallas Bible Church; www.leaderu.com/orgs/probe/docs/worship.html

[24] **Gibbs,** <u>Worship</u>

life, when, in truth, it was He who had fit me into His Life. It is so easy to make God a convenience, like a good friend next door; being there when we need Him, but not bothering us otherwise. This is entirely wrong. The solution is to spend time with God daily in meditation and devotion.

If not '*missing,*' as Bro. Tozer said, 'true worship' has certainly diminished greatly in the present Laodicean Church Age of ease and convenience. It seems there is little time or thought, anymore, for the sincere *worship* of the living God. It seems that we have, indeed, *lost the wonder* of our wonderful God.

Charles Spurgeon reproves us

"Many may be met with who know God, but never glorify him as God, because they never adore him, and worship him, with the love of their hearts. They go to church or to some place of worship regularly, and sing psalms and hymns, and they may even have family-prayer at home; but their heart has never adored the living God with living love. Their worship has a name to live, but it is dead. They present to the Lord all the eternal harvest of worship, but the corn is gone, only the straw and the husk are there. And what is the value of your husky prayers? your prayers without a kernel, made up of the straw of words, and the chaff of formality? What is the value of professions of loyalty from a rebel? What is the worth of professed friendship to God when your heart is at enmity against him? Is it not a mockery of God to present to him a sacrifice "where not the heart is found?" When the Lord has to say— They come as my people, and they sit as my people, and they sing as my people, but their heart is far from me,— can he take any pleasure in them? May not God thus complain of many? Oh, let it not be so with you! I know that there are some here against whom that charge would lie if we preferred it— that they know God, but they do not glorify him as God, for they do not love him. The name and service of God are much on their tongues, but they do not delight in him, they do not hunger and thirst after him, they do not find prayer and praise to be their very element, but such service as they render is merely lip-service, the unwilling homage of bond-slaves, and not the delighted service of those who are the children of God. Oh, my brethren, if we accept Jehovah as the living God, let us give him the utmost love of our souls. Will you call a man brother, and then treat him like a dog? Dare you call God your God, and then act towards him as though he were not worthy of a thought. With what joy does David cry, "I am thy servant, and the son of thine handmaid: thou hast loosed my bonds!" This is the kind of spirit with which to deal with the Lord. Oh, to rejoice in God all the day, and to make him our exceeding joy! Thus, and thus only, do we glorify him as God. Without the fire of love no incense will ever rise from the censer of praise. If we do not delight in God we do not fitly adore God."[25]

Warren W. Wiersbe adds

"Most Christians are too busy to worship, and many church services are so filled with man-made promotion that God is almost forgotten. People go to church to be spectators at a religious program, not participants in spiritual worship. They spend their time in counting, not weighing! As long as there are 'results' nobody cares whether or not God was pleased as His people gathered to honor Him and offer Him spiritual worship... the missing ingredient is worship... ascribing to God worth and not 'using God' to produce the results we have already planned."[26]

Purpose of worship

A.P. Gibbs says

"[A] great deal of confusion exists in Christendom as to just what constitutes worship.

---

[25] **C.H. Spurgeon**, Knowledge— Worship— Gratitude

[26] **Warren Wiersbe**, Real Worship

"The term, 'worship,' like many other great words, such as 'grace' and 'love,' defies adequate definition. The meaning of these words, like the exquisite perfume of a rose, or the delightful flavor of honey, is more easily experienced than described." [27]

Dr. Peter Ruckman adds

"Worship is different from prayer and praise; for example, 'Lord, save my soul' or 'Lord, give me this' can be a prayer. 'Thank you, Lord, for saving my soul,' is praise, or, 'Thank you, Lord,' for whatever the Lord has given you, is praise. But worship is thanking God for what He is. Worshipping is adoring God as a living person, a living being, an Almighty Creator who is God of gods, King of kings, Lord of lords, the Almighty, the Everlasting, the Alpha and Omega, the Beginning and the Ending.

"The first mention of the word 'worship' in the Bible occurs in Genesis 22:5, which tells us plainly that true worship is always connected with a blood sacrifice. Abraham tells his men, 'I and the lad will go yonder and worship, and come again to you' (Genesis 22:5). The fact that he believed he and the boy were both coming back shows that Abraham believed in resurrection. So the first time worship occurs in the Bible it is connected with Isaac, a type of Christ; a blood atonement, typified by a lamb; and the resurrection of a dead son.

"In Matthew 2:2 the wise men came to worship the newborn king, Jesus Christ; so, the first time the word 'worship' occurs in the New Testament, it is connected with the birth of Jesus Christ... a Jewish king.

"Worship means 'to do reverence or homage to a superior being.' Men ought to worship God because He is God...

"Worship is the uprising of a heart that has known the Father as a Giver, the Son as Saviour, and the Holy Spirit

---

[27] **A.P. Gibbs**, Worship: The Christian's Highest Occupation, (Walterick Publishers, P.O. Box 2216, Kansas City, Kansas 66110 USA) ISBN 0-937396-57-5. This is a classic work on worship.

as the indwelling Comforter. Worship is the occupation of the heart, not with its needs, or even with its blessings. Worship is the occupation of the heart with God Himself...

"The importance of worship cannot be overestimated or overstated. It is the First Commandment of the Law. The Lord said, 'Thou shalt have no other gods before me' (Exodus 20:3). Jesus Christ Himself said, 'The first of all the commandments is, Hear, O Israel; the Lord our God is one Lord: And thou shalt love the Lord thy God with all thy heart, and with all thy soul, and with all thy mind, and with all thy strength: This is the first commandment' (Mark 12:29-30), not the second commandment.

"There are many hindrances to worship. Worship is the Christian's highest occupation and is therefore contested by Satan. Satan will do everything he can to keep you talking about 'the Holy Ghost' and 'the gifts of the Holy Ghost,' instead of worshipping God. Satan will do everything he can to make you think that Sunday morning worship service is the time to worship God, and the rest of the time is a time to enjoy yourself.

➲ The first hindrance to worship is 'SELF WILL'...

➲ 'WORLDLINESS' hinders worship...

➲ 'A CRITICAL SPIRIT' hinders true worship...

➲ Some people are just too 'LAZY' to exert the energy needed to worship God...

➲ 'IMPATIENCE' hinders worship...

➲ 'FORMALISM' is a terrible hindrance to true worship...

➲ 'PRIDE'...

"May there rise from every Christian's heart a constant flow of adoring worship which will delight the heart of God and bring glory to His holy name. He alone is worthy to be praised, a great King of kings, God of gods, Lord of lords, the Alpha and Omega, the Beginning and Ending, the Lord Jesus Christ, the Way, the Truth, the Life, the Door, the Bread of Life, the Water of Life, the Rose of Sharon, the Lily of the Valley, the Altogether Lovely One, the King of Israel, the Messiah, the Christ, the Anointed of God, my Saviour, my God, my Beloved and my Friend. May His name be praised for ever and ever. Amen and Amen."[28]

Andrew Murray instructs us further

"There can be no true worship or drawing nigh to God except as we are like-minded to Christ, and come with His Spirit and disposition in us...

"Man belongs to two worlds; the visible and the invisible.

"In the Old testament worship, the external was the more prominent. It consisted mostly in carnal ordinances, imposed until a time of reformation. They taught a measure of truth, they exercised a certain influence on the heart, but they could not make the worshipper perfect. It was only with the New Testament that the religion of the inner life, the worship of God 'in spirit and in truth' (John 4:23-24), was revealed.

"With A True Heart

"In man's nature the heart is the central power. As the heart is, so is the man. The desire and the choice, the love and the hatred of the heart prove what a man is already, and decide what he is to become. Just as we judge of a man's physical character, his size and strength and age and habits, by his outward appearance, so the heart gives the real inward man his character; and 'the hidden man of the heart' is what God looks to. God has in Christ given us access to the secret place of His dwelling, to the inner sanctuary of His presence and His heart; no wonder the first thing He asks, as He calls us unto Him, is

---

[28] **Peter S. Ruckman,** Theological Studies— Vol. 1

the heart— a true heart; our inmost being must in truth be yielded to Him, true to Him.

"True religion is a thing of the heart, an inward life. It is only as the desire of the heart is fixed upon God, the whole heart seeking for God, giving its love and finding its joy in God, that a man can draw near to God... As far as Christ through His Spirit is within the heart, making the thoughts and will likeminded with Himself, so far can a man's worship and service be acceptable to God...

"God asks for the heart. Alas, how many Christians serve Him still with the service of the old covenant! There are seasons for Bible-reading and praying and church-going. But when one notices how speedily and naturally and happily, as soon as it is freed from restraint, the heart turns to worldly things, one feels how little there is of the heart in it; it is not the worship of a true heart, of the whole heart...

"And what may be the reason that so few Christians can testify of the joy and the power of a heart at all times sprinkled from an evil conscience? The answer is, that in the apprehension of this, as of every other truth, there are stages according to the measure of faith and faithfulness. See it in Israel. There you have three stages.

1. The Israelite, who entered the outer court, saw the altar and the blood sprinkled there, and received such assurance of pardon as that could give him.

2. The priest, who was admitted to the Holy Place, not only saw the blood sprinkled on the brazen altar, he had it sprinkled upon himself, and might see it sprinkled on the golden altar in the Holy Place. His contact with the blood was closer, and he was admitted to a nearer access.

3. The access of the High Priest was still more complete; he might, with the blood for the mercy-seat, once a year enter within the veil.

1. Even so, there are OUTER-COURT CHRISTIANS, who trust in Christ who died on Calvary, but know very little of His heavenly life, or near access to God, or service for others.

2. Beyond these, there are Christians who know that they are called to be priests, and to live in the service of God and their fellow-men. They know more of the power of the blood as setting apart for service; but yet their life is still without the veil.

3. But then come those who know what Christ's entering with His blood implies and procures, and who experience that the Holy Spirit applies the blood in such power, that it indeed brings to the life in the inner sanctuary, in the full and abiding joy of God's presence.

"Let us draw near, with a true heart, in fulness of faith, having our hearts sprinkled from an evil conscience. Oh, let us not bring reproach upon the blood of the Lamb by not believing in its power to give us perfect access to God. Let us listen and hear them sing without ceasing the praise of the blood of the Lamb in heaven; as we trust and honour and rejoice in it, we shall enter the heaven of God's presence."[29]

Psalm 46:10 is a wonderful verse to instruct us in simple worship

"BE STILL, and KNOW that I am God: I will be exalted among the heathen, I WILL BE EXALTED in the earth."   — Psalms 46:10

"Be still;" how foreign are these words to the mind of modern man, who is constantly *driven* by the world, the flesh and the devil. Obedience to this command will only come from the believer who stands in AWE at the power and majesty of God.

---

[29] **Andrew Murray**, The Holiest of All, A Devotional Exposition of the Epistle to the Hebrews, from the exposition of chapter 10, verses 19-25.

Firstly: When He says "Be still," He does not mean for us just to be inanimate, physically. He means, moreover, for us to "be quiet" in our inner being; to withdraw from worldly care; to put away all fears and strife of this life.

A.W. Tozer observes

> "Unquestionably, part of our failure today is religious activity that is not preceded by aloneness, by inactivity. I mean getting alone with God and waiting in silence and quietness until we are charged with God's Spirit. Then, when we act, our activity really amounts to something because we have been prepared by God for it..." [30]

Remember how the Lord Jesus Christ commanded the raging winds and waves in the midst of the storm on the Sea of Galilee. As the Master of the sea spoke, the wind and waves became still and quiet, for even nature is still at the voice of the Creator.

As the apostle John found as he lay his head on the breast of Christ at the last supper (John 13:23), so He wants us to know the peace and rest of one who hears the very heartbeat of God. There, in that stillness, we will find that meditation is sweet (Psalm 104:34), as He reveals Himself to us as the Lord of glory. Just as He stilled the tempest on the sea, Christ stilled the tempest in John's heart that must have arisen when He revealed that one of the twelve apostles would betray Him. In the midst of tragic revelation, John knew "the peace of God, that passeth all understanding" (Philippians 4:7), as he obeyed the divine imperative "draw nigh to God, and He will draw nigh to you" (James 4:8).

Secondly: The Lord continues; "and know that I am God" (Psalm 46:10) When God instructs us to "know," it is because He is about to reveal something to us. Anyone can know *about* God by reading the Bible. But the only ones who can *know* Him, are those to whom He reveals Himself by the Holy Spirit. Nevertheless, it only when we lay aside this sinful body of flesh and have our new glorified body shall we know Him perfectly.

---

[30] **A.W. Tozer**, <u>Faith Beyond Reason</u>, pp. 130,133

<u>As Paul the Apostle writes</u>

> **"For now we see through a glass, darkly; but then face to face: now I know in part; but then shall I know even as also I am known."**   **— I Corinthians 13:12**

Until then, we can only "know in part," but, oh, the glory that we see in part is more than we can contain. And what shall it be in that day (Zechariah 14:9) that John the Apostle declares?

> **"Beloved, now are we the sons of God, and it doth not yet appear what we shall be: but we know that, when he shall appear, we shall be like him; for we shall see him as he is."**   **— I John 3:2**

<u>See how the Psalmist worships the Lord:</u>

> **"Make a joyful noise unto the LORD, all ye lands.**
>
> **Serve the LORD with gladness: come before his presence with singing.**
>
> **KNOW YE THAT THE LORD HE IS GOD: it is he that hath made us, and not we ourselves; we are his people, and the sheep of his pasture.**
>
> **"Enter into his gates with thanksgiving, and into his courts with praise: be thankful unto him, and bless his name.**
>
> **"For the LORD is good; his mercy is everlasting; and his truth endureth to all generations."**
>
>   **— Psalms 100:1-5**

The knowledge that the Lord is God should move our hearts to praise Him for who He is. And how can we know that He is God, except by faith?

<u>A.P. Gibbs says again</u>

> "We learn, first, that *worship is based on a revelation from God.* (cf. Genesis 22:1,2). *'And God said.'* It was in response to a word from God that Abraham acted. It was not something he thought up himself, but was his

response to a Divine revelation. *Faith always presupposes a previous revelation.* We are told that: *'Faith cometh by hearing, and hearing by the WORD of God'* (Romans 10:17). For one to act without Divine authority is presumption in the worst degree. Take faith away from Abraham's act in offering up Isaac, and it becomes murder! The WORSHIP of the Lord, as also the WORK of the Lord, must be guided by the WORD of the Lord. The believer's authority in worship is not the traditions of men, however hoary with antiquity, nor the subtle reasonings of human wisdom, however plausible; but the clear *revelation of God's word.*" [31]

The Bible tells us

"But without FAITH it is impossible to please him: for he that cometh to God must believe that he is, and that he is a rewarder of them that diligently seek him."   — Hebrews 11:6

➲ There is no worship without faith;

➲ And there is no faith apart from revelation. [32]

"So then FAITH cometh by hearing, and hearing by the word of God."   — Romans 10:17

"But as it is written, Eye hath not seen, nor ear heard, neither have entered into the heart of man, the things which God hath prepared for them that love him.

"But God hath REVEALED them unto us by his Spirit: for the Spirit searcheth all things, yea, the deep things of God."
                                        — I Corinthians 2:9-10

---

[31] **A.P. Gibbs**, Worship

[32] See Faith— It Works by **Linton M. Smith Jr.** for fuller development of this subject.

> **"The secret of the LORD is with them that fear him;
> and he will shew them his covenant." — Psalms 25:14**

Years ago A.W. Tozer wrote a book titled <u>God Tells the Man Who Cares</u>. I wonder, what would God tell us if we would fall in love with Him and worship Him everyday? We must take time to meditate on God Himself, and on His word. Then, the Lord will reveal Himself to us in a very real and personal way. As we are in perfect communion with Him, we will understand the meaning of true worship.

Thirdly: In the words "I will be exalted" (Psalm 46:10), we see that **the purpose of worship is to exalt the Lord as God.**

<u>The Psalmist writes again</u>

> **"My heart is fixed, O God, my heart is fixed: I will sing and give praise.**
>
> **"Awake up, my glory; awake, psaltery and harp: I myself will awake early.**
>
> **"I will praise thee, O Lord, among the people: I will sing unto thee among the nations.**
>
> **"For thy mercy is great unto the heavens, and thy truth unto the clouds.**
>
> **"BE THOU EXALTED O GOD, above the heavens: let thy glory be above all the earth."**
> **— Psalms 57:7-11**

The name of the Lord Jesus Christ is above every name; it is glorious, and is exalted above all blessing and praise and full of majesty.

> **"[S]tand up and bless the LORD your God for ever and ever: and blessed be THY GLORIOUS NAME, which is exalted above all blessing and praise."**
> **— Nehemiah 9:5b**

> **"Who being the brightness of his glory, and the express image of his person, and upholding all things by the word of his power, when he had by himself**

purged our sins, sat down on the right hand of the Majesty on high;" [33]   **— Hebrews 1:3**

"Wherefore God also hath highly exalted him, and given him A NAME which is ABOVE EVERY NAME:"   **— Philippians 2:9**

I am reminded of Jack Hayford's song about the majesty of God

MAJESTY
"Majesty, worship His Majesty.
Unto Jesus, be all glory, honor and praise!
Majesty, kingdom authority,
Flow from His throne, unto His own
His anthem raise.

"So exalt, lift up on high the name of Jesus.
Magnify, come glorify Christ Jesus, the King!
Majesty, worship His Majesty,
Jesus, who died, now glorified,
King of all Kings!"

That brings to mind another hymn of praise to His name.

ALL HAIL THE POWER OF JESUS NAME
"All hail the power of Jesus' name!
Let angels prostrate fall;
Bring forth the royal diadem,
And crown Him lord of all.

"Ye chosen seed of Israel's race
A remnant weak and small,
Hail him who saves you by His grace
And crown Him Lord of all.

---

[33] Throughout scripture, the position at the "right hand" is the place of honor and power.

"Let every kindred, every tribe
On this terrestrial ball,
To Him all majesty ascribe,
And crown Him Lord of all.

"O that with yonder sacred throng
We at His feet may fall,
Join in the everlasting song,
And crown Him Lord of all."

In the presence of God there is constant worship.

"In the year that king Uzziah died I saw also the Lord sitting upon a throne, high and lifted up, and his train filled the temple.

"Above it stood the seraphims: each one had six wings; with twain he covered his face, and with twain he covered his feet, and with twain he did fly.

"And one cried unto another, and said, Holy, holy, holy, is the LORD of hosts: the whole earth is full of his glory."

— Isaiah 6:1-3

"And the four beasts had each of them six wings about him; and they were full of eyes within: and they rest not day and night, saying, Holy, holy, holy, Lord God Almighty, which was, and is, and is to come.

"And when those beasts give glory and honour and thanks to him that sat on the throne, who liveth for ever and ever,

"The four and twenty elders fall down before him that sat on the throne, and worship him that liveth for ever and ever, and cast their crowns before the throne, saying,

"Thou art worthy, O Lord, to receive glory and honour and power: for thou hast created all things, and for thy pleasure they are and were created."

— Revelation 4:8-11

The Old Testament scene of Isaiah had not changed when John viewed it from the Isle of Patmos as he wrote the Book of Revelation; neither has it changed today. Before the throne of God, there is constant worship of God, not only because of what He has done, but because of who He is.

NOW, we worship Him by faith, but THEN all will worship Him simply because they cannot do otherwise; for worship is the natural response of the regenerated soul in the presence of the power and glory of God Almighty.

We must never forget where we are in history. Ours is the time of the church of Laodicea and we must realize our offense to God.

> "And unto the angel of the church of the Laodiceans write; These things saith the Amen, the faithful and true witness, the beginning of the creation of God;
>
> "I KNOW THY WORKS, that thou art neither cold nor hot: I would thou wert cold or hot.
>
> "So then because THOU ART LUKEWARM, and neither cold nor hot, I will spue thee out of my mouth.
>
> "BECAUSE THOU SAYEST, I am rich, and increased with goods, and have need of nothing; and knowest not that thou art wretched, and miserable, and poor, and blind, and naked:
>
> "I COUNSEL THEE to buy of me gold tried in the fire, that thou mayest be rich; and white raiment, that thou mayest be clothed, and that the shame of thy nakedness do not appear; and anoint thine eyes with eyesalve, that thou mayest see.
>
> "As many as I love, I rebuke and chasten: BE ZEALOUS therefore, and REPENT."
>
> — Revelation 3:14-19

We must resist the temptation to try to worship God in any manner after the flesh (remember Cain— Genesis 4:3; Jude 1:11). God is more interested in "quality" (holiness) than "quantity" (numbers). Many "worship" services have become nothing more than Christian "entertainment" services. Some have even created a "night club" environment with tables, chairs, dim lighting and a spotlight on the featured "celebrity" performer. Yes, we can bring more people into our services, but to what end? This kind of carnal appeal only degrades our concept of God. It was to this very sort of thing that Moses descended from Mt. Sinai (Exodus 32:17-18). What would he have thought if he had come down to a "rock gospel music" concert today? No doubt, Joshua would have thought it "the NOISE of war."

We cannot bring the music of the world into the church, put some Christian words to it and expect God to receive it as worship. Of course, our flesh might like it, but it would be contrary to the Spirit.

> **"For the flesh lusteth against the Spirit, and the Spirit against the flesh: and these are contrary the one to the other: so that ye cannot do the things that ye would."** — **Galatians 5:17**

> **"For we... worship God in the spirit, and rejoice in Christ Jesus, and have no confidence in the flesh."** — **Philippians 3:3**

As part of our worship, our music must be spiritual.

> **"Speaking to yourselves in psalms and hymns and spiritual songs, singing and making melody in your heart to the Lord;"** — **Ephesians 5:19**

It is not a grand "performance" that is important, but "singing and making melody in your heart to the Lord" that counts. Exalting the Lord stirs our spirit to sing and make melody in our hearts, then "out of the abundance of the heart the mouth speaketh" (Luke 6:45). Thereby our lips give praise to His glorious name.

While we are never to forsake assembling together for worship and preaching (Hebrews 10:25), we can worship Him day by day in our hearts wherever we are. We must spend time alone with the Lord. Worship is never more pure than when we are alone with God.

Thomas Jefferson said simply

"Worship requires only a man and God."
— Thomas Jefferson

That is true whether we are alone or gathered together in a building filled with people. For in the end, each man stands alone before God as His own priest to worship Him. We do not have to have a Catholic priest, idols, beautiful architecture and a grandiose ceremony to worship God in spirit and in truth. But we must have Him.

We see revealed in the Proverbs, worship in its simplest form.

"Trust in the LORD with all thine heart; and lean not unto thine own understanding.

In all thy ways acknowledge him, and he shall direct thy paths."
— Proverbs 3:5-6

The Bible says

"Acquaint now thyself with him, and be at peace: thereby good shall come unto thee.

"Receive, I pray thee, the law from his mouth, and lay up his words in thine heart.

"For then shalt thou have thy delight in the Almighty, and shalt lift up thy face unto God."
— Job 22:21-22, 26

When we are on intimate terms with the Lord of Glory, we will *"delight in the Almighty"* and give Him the worship due Him.

➲ **First,** we delight in the worship of the Lord Jesus Christ because it gives Him the GLORY due His name.

"Let them PRAISE the name of the LORD: for his name alone is excellent; his glory is above the earth and heaven."   **— Psalms 148:13**

"Give unto the LORD the GLORY due unto his name; WORSHIP the LORD in the beauty of holiness."
— Psalm 29:2

Here is another wonderful hymn about the glory of His name.

GLORY TO HIS NAME

"Down at the cross where my Savior died,
Down where for cleansing from sin I cried,
There to my heart was the blood applied;
Glory to His Name!

"I am so wondrously saved from sin,
Jesus so sweetly abides within;
There at the cross where He took me in;
Glory to His Name!

"Oh, precious fountain that saves from sin,
I am so glad I have entered in;
There Jesus saves me and keeps me clean;
Glory to His Name!

"Come to this fountain so rich and sweet,
Cast thy poor soul at the Savior's feet;
Plunge in today, and be made complete;
Glory to His Name!

Chorus:
"Glory to His Name, glory to His Name:
There to my heart was the blood applied;
Glory to His Name!"

The Bible says

"THOU ART WORTHY, O Lord, to receive glory and honour and power: for thou hast created all things, and for thy pleasure they are and were created."
                                        — Revelation 4:11

Let us be careful to remember Who He is and what He has done. He is worthy, therefore let us give Him "glory and honour and power," because that is why we were created. One sure sign of a born again Christian is His praise for His Savior. It is the natural expression of adoration from one who has received His spirit. If our hearts are filled with Christ, we cannot do otherwise.

"Let the heaven and earth praise him, the seas, and every thing that moveth therein."   **— Psalms 69:34**

"Every day will I bless thee; and I will praise thy name for ever and ever."   **— Psalms 145:2**

"Let every thing that hath breath praise the LORD. Praise ye the LORD."   **— Psalms 150:6**

"But when the Comforter is come, whom I will send unto you from the Father, even the Spirit of truth, which proceedeth from the Father, he shall testify of me:"   **— John 15:26**

Here is part of a message A.W. Tozer preached

"The Act of Worship

"There are ingredients that make up worship. One is ADMIRATION. We can admire without worshipping but we cannot worship without admiring, because worship is admiration carried to infinitude.

"In the same way, we can honor what we do not worship but we cannot worship the one we do not honor. So worship carries with it an ingredient of HONOR.

"Then there is the spirit we call FASCINATION. We can only worship that which fascinates us. The old poet said in an often quoted passage, 'In our astonished reverence, we confess Thy uncreated loveliness.' There is an astonishment about reverence. If you can explain it, you cannot worship it. You may admire it, you may honor it, but there is a mysterious fascination that carries the heart beyond itself and then we are nearer to worship.

"Another ingredient, which perhaps should have been mentioned first, is LOVE. We can love without worshipping but we cannot worship without loving. Then love, when it lets itself go and no longer has any restraints, becomes adoration.

"We need to refine our definitions. Such words as honor, love and adore don't mean what they are supposed to mean. We use divine language in such a common way that when we try to rise to the exalted and divine level we find ourselves using words that do not express anything. If I had the power, I would pass a law permitting the use of such words as love, honor and adore only in prayer, Bible teaching, preaching and song. We have spoiled them and made them common, yet they belong to God.

"Worship seeks union with its beloved, and an active effort to close the gap between the heart and the God it adores is worship at its best."[34]

➲ **Second,** we delight in the worship of the Lord Jesus Christ because it shows our LOVE for Him.

> **"Let all those that seek thee rejoice and be glad in thee: let such as love thy salvation say continually, The LORD be magnified."** — Psalms 40:16

Another sure sign of a real born again Christian is his LOVE for God. The psalmist says there are certain characteristics of those who seek to know the Lord; they rejoice and are glad in Him. And,

---

[34] **A.W. Tozer,** "The Act and Art of Worship," a pamphlet.

those who love His salvation have something to say, even when they don't know what to say; "The Lord be magnified." We should say it and hear it from other believers "continually." We often say "[P]raise the Lord!" as well.

> **"But if any man love God, the same is known of him."**   **— I Corinthians 8:3**

If we are filled with the Spirit of God and truly love our God, everyone will know; it cannot be hidden. How many people know you are a Christian because of your love for God? Are you a secret disciple?

> **"We love him, because he first loved us."**
>   **— I John 4:19**

Here is the expression of God's love

> **"For God so loved the world, that he gave his only begotten Son, that whosoever believeth in him should not perish, but have everlasting life."**   **— John 3:16**

If He loved us that much, how much should we love Him and "His salvation" that He paid for at such a great price. But, don't say you love Him if you will not obey Him.

> **"For this is the love of God, that we keep his commandments: and his commandments are not grievous."**   **— I John 5:3**

I just could not go on without inserting the following great old hymn about a believer's love for God.

MY JESUS, I LOVE THEE

"My Jesus, I love Thee, I know Thou art mine;
For Thee all the follies of sin I resign.
My gracious Redeemer, my Savior art Thou
If ever I loved Thee, my Jesus, 'tis now.

"I love Thee because Thou has first loved me,
And purchased my pardon on Calvary's tree.
I love Thee for wearing the thorns on Thy brow;
If ever I loved Thee, my Jesus, 'tis now.

"I'll love Thee in life, I will love Thee in death,
And praise Thee as long as Thou lendest me breath;
And say when the death dew lies cold on my brow,
If ever I loved Thee, my Jesus, 'tis now.

"In mansions of glory and endless delight,
I'll ever adore Thee in heaven so bright;
I'll sing with the glittering crown on my brow;
If ever I loved Thee, my Jesus, 'tis now."

➲ **Third,** we delight in the worship of the Lord Jesus Christ because it demonstrates our SUBMISSION unto Him.

In our worship of the Lord Jesus Christ, we must submit unto His authority, but what a simple thing it is to submit unto Him. Therefore, let us gladly bow down before Him and no other. In our submission, others should see that He is our God.

"O come, let us worship and BOW down: let us KNEEL before the LORD our maker."   — Psalms 95:6

"EXALT ye the Lord our God, and WORSHIP at his footstool; for he is holy."   — Psalm 99:5

"All the earth shall WORSHIP thee, and shall SING unto thee; they shall sing to thy name. Selah."

— Psalm 66:4

"For this cause I bow my knees unto the Father of our Lord Jesus Christ,"   — Ephesians 3:14

"For it is written, As I live, saith the Lord, every knee shall bow to me, and every tongue shall confess to God."   — **Romans 14:11**

<u>God hates idolatry!</u>

The Lord commands us not to bow before, nor serve, any graven image. Only the Lord Jesus Christ is worthy of our worship.

    ⊃ We WILL NOT bow to the Pope,

    ⊃ We WILL NOT bow to Mary,

    ⊃ We WILL NOT bow to Peter

    ⊃ And we WILL NOT bow to any other idol

<u>God spoke clearly about this</u>

"Thou shalt not make unto thee any graven image, or any likeness of any thing that is in heaven above, or that is in the earth beneath, or that is in the water under the earth:

"Thou shalt not bow down thyself to them, nor serve them: for I the LORD thy God am a jealous God, visiting the iniquity of the fathers upon the children unto the third and fourth generation of them that hate me;"

        — **Exodus 20:4-5**

In Revelation 22:9 (cf. 19:10), John the apostle bowed before an angel, who reproved him. The angel told John not to bow to him, for he was no more worthy of worship than the prophets, nor his brethren who believed in Christ. The angel's final instruction was— **"worship God."**

"And I John saw these things, and heard them. And when I had heard and seen, I fell down to worship before the feet of the angel which shewed me these things.

"Then saith he unto me, See thou do it not: for I am thy fellowservant, and of thy brethren the prophets, and of them which keep the sayings of this book: worship God."

— Revelation 22:8-9

Neither would the apostle Peter allow anyone to worship him.

"And as Peter was coming in, Cornelius met him, and fell down at his feet, and worshipped him.

"But Peter took him up, saying, Stand up; I myself also am a man."

— Acts 10:25-26

⮑ **Fourth,** we delight in the worship of **the Lord Jesus Christ** because it is a TESTIMONY to the world that He is God.

"Know ye that the LORD he is God: it is he that hath made us, and not we ourselves; we are his people, and the sheep of his pasture."   — Psalms 100:3

"But ye are a chosen generation, a royal priesthood, an holy nation, a peculiar people; that ye should shew forth the praises of him who hath called you out of darkness into his marvellous light:"   — I Peter 2:9

"I will WORSHIP toward thy holy temple, and PRAISE thy name for thy lovingkindness and for thy truth: for thou hast magnified thy word above all thy name."   — Psalm 138:2

"Declare his glory among the heathen; his marvellous works among all nations."   — I Chronicles 16:24

Preparation to Worship

Before we can come before the Lord in 'sincere worship,' we must **prepare our hearts**. True worship begins when we commune with God, and we cannot commune with Him until our hearts are fully in agreement with His own heart (Amos 3:3).

1. The first element in preparation to worship the Lord is to SEEK HIM IN PRAYER.

> **"If thou prepare thine heart, and stretch out thine hands toward him;"**   **— Job 11:13**

That is a man in prayer. The preparation of the heart comes by meditating on the word of God and magnifying the name of the Lord.

> **"LORD, thou hast heard the desire of the humble: thou wilt prepare their heart, thou wilt cause thine ear to hear:"**   **— Psalms 10:17**

That also is a man in prayer. If we will prepare our hearts to meet Him, God will take up where we leave off and make a deeper preparation as only the Spirit of God could. We make much of 'words,' but God knows our heart and hears the desire of our heart.

> **"Likewise the Spirit also helpeth our infirmities: for we know not what we should pray for as we ought: but the Spirit itself maketh intercession for us with groanings which cannot be uttered.**
>
> **"And he that searcheth the hearts knoweth what is the mind of the Spirit, because he maketh intercession for the saints according to the will of God."**
>
> **— Romans 8:26-27**

We read in the book of James

> **"But he giveth more grace. Wherefore he saith, God resisteth the proud, but giveth grace unto the humble.**

"Be afflicted, and mourn, and weep: let your laugh-
ter be turned to mourning, and your joy to heaviness.

"Humble yourselves in the sight of the Lord, and he
shall lift you up."

— James 4:6, 9-10

"The LORD is nigh unto them that are of a broken
heart; and saveth such as be of a contrite spirit."

— Psalms 34:18

God's response to our preparation and our prayers is communion of the Holy Spirit with the seeker, then the Spirit makes intercession "according to the will of God." Part of the preparation is to
find the will of God and to bring our will in line with His.

"Draw nigh to God, and he will draw nigh to you..."

— James 4:8

I said at first "[Before] we can come before the Lord in 'sincere
worship,' because much that passes for worship today is not true
worship at all. It is merely a time to enjoy religious entertainment
centered around worldly 'Christian' music (so-called). We have
now adapted our worship services to suit all lifestyles, so the services won't offend even the unsaved. Having carefully learned the
right Bible terminology to describe our religious experience, we
appear still to be worshipping God.

"This know also, that in THE LAST DAYS perilous
times shall come.

"For men shall be lovers of their own selves, covet-
ous, boasters, proud, blasphemers, disobedient to
parents, unthankful, unholy,

"Without natural affection, trucebreakers, false
accusers, incontinent, fierce, despisers of those that
are good,

"Traitors, heady, highminded, lovers of pleasures
more than lovers of God;

"Having <u>a form of godliness</u>, but denying the power thereof: from such turn away.

"For of this sort are they which creep into houses, and lead captive silly women laden with sins, led away with divers lusts,

"Ever learning, and <u>never able to come to the knowledge of the truth</u>.

"Now as Jannes and Jambres withstood Moses, so do <u>these also resist the truth</u>: men of corrupt minds, reprobate concerning the faith.

"But they shall proceed no further: for <u>their folly shall be manifest unto all men</u>, as theirs also was."

— II Timothy 3:1-9

In many churches where we were once invited to *worship*, we are now invited to join a *celebration*. From what I know of the Laodicean church, there is not much justification for *celebration* until we have our priorities in order. It seems that in all our celebrating, we have lost the manifestation of His presence in our services, because we have lost the manifestation of His Spirit, through holiness, in our lives.

"Behold, I stand at the door, and knock: if any man hear my voice, and open the door, I will come in to him, and will sup with him, and he with me."

— Revelation 3:20

We sometimes use this verse in witnessing to the unsaved; that is fine, because it is a spiritual application of the verse. However, doctrinally it is for the Church. We find them feeling they have need of nothing. They have teaching, celebration, music and everything one could desire for a religious service, except the presence of Christ Himself. We are leaning on the arm of the flesh, and it shall fail us. All our preparation and prayer is in vain unless we remember that *every* service must be centered around the Lord Jesus Christ. It is the responsibility of each individual believer to open the door of his heart and invite Him to be the honored guest and master of the house.

2. A second element in preparation of our hearts to worship God, is to FORSAKE THE WORLD AND ALL ITS PLEASURES.

> "For all that is in the world, the lust of the flesh, and the lust of the eyes, and the pride of life, is not of the Father, but is of the world."   — I John 2:16

> "Ye adulterers and adulteresses, know ye not that the friendship of the world is enmity with God? whosoever therefore will be a friend of the world is the enemy of God."   — James 4:4

A.W. Tozer reproves us with these words

"The Christian who gazes too long on the carnal pleasures of this world cannot escape a certain feeling of sympathy with them, and that feeling will inevitably lead to behavior that is worldly. To expose our hearts to truth and consistently refuse or neglect to obey the impulses it arouses is to stymie the motions of life within us, and if persisted in, to grieve the Holy Spirit into silence."[35]

"[T]o sow (to the flesh) is our privilege— if we want to reap the harvest of corruption which must inevitably follow (a harvest no man in his right mind could deliberately choose). No, the snare lies in choosing the pleasures of sowing with the secret hope that in some way we can escape the sorrows of the reaping; but never since the beginning of the world has it been possible to separate the one from the other."[36]

"I am perfectly certain that I could rake up fifteen boxcar loads of fundamentalist Christians this hour in the city of Chicago who are more influenced in their whole outlook by Hollywood than they are by the Lord Jesus Christ. I am positive that much that passes for the gospel in our day is very little more than a very mild case of

---

[35] **A.W. Tozer**, Renewed Day By Day, April 21 reading

[36] **A.W. Tozer**, The Next Chapter After the Last, p.87

orthodox religion grafted on to a heart that is sold out to the world in its pleasures and tastes and ambitions." [37]

"No one with common human feeling will object to the simple pleasures of life, nor to such harmless forms of entertainment as may help to relax the nerves and refresh the mind exhausted by toil. Such things if used with discretion may be a blessing along the way. That is one thing. The all-out devotion to entertainment as a major activity for which and by which men live is definitely something else again.

"The abuse of a harmless thing is the essence of sin. The growth of the amusement phase of human life to such fantastic proportions is a portent, a threat to the souls of modern men. It has been built into a multimillion dollar racket with greater power over human minds and human character than any other educational influence on earth. And the ominous thing is that its power is almost exclusively evil, rotting the inner life, crowding out the long eternal thoughts which would fill the souls of men if they were but worthy to entertain them. And the whole thing has grown into a veritable religion which holds its devotees with a strange fascination, and a religion, incidentally, against which it is now dangerous to speak.

"For centuries the Church stood solidly against every form of worldly entertainment, recognizing it for what it was— a device for wasting time, a refuge from the disturbing voice of conscience, a scheme to divert attention from moral accountability. For this she got herself abused roundly by the sons of this world. But of late she has become tired of the abuse and has given over the struggle. She appears to have decided that if she cannot conquer the great god 'Entertainment' she may as well join forces with him and make what use she can of his powers. So today we have the astonishing spectacle of millions of dollars being poured into the unholy job of providing earthly entertainment for the so-called sons of heaven. Religious entertainment is in many places rapidly

---

[37] **A.W. Tozer**, <u>How to Be Filled With the Holy Spirit</u>, p.52

crowding out the serious things of God. Many churches these days have become little more than poor theaters where fifth-rate 'producers' peddle their shoddy wares with the full approval of evangelical leaders who can even quote a holy text in defense of their delinquency. And hardly a man dares raise his voice against it.

"The great god 'Entertainment' amuses his devotees mainly by telling them stories. The love of stories, which is a characteristic of childhood, has taken fast hold of the minds of the retarded saints of our day, so much so that not a few persons manage to make a comfortable living by spinning yarns and serving them up in various disguises to church people. What is natural and beautiful in a child may be shocking when it persists into adulthood, and more so when it appears in the sanctuary and seeks to pass for true religion.

"Is it not a strange thing and a wonder that, with the shadow of atomic destruction hanging over the world and with the coming of Christ drawing near, the professed followers of the Lord should be giving themselves up to religious amusements? That in an hour when mature saints are so desperately needed, vast numbers of believers should revert to spiritual childhood and clamor for religious toys?"[38]

We should mourn the decline of our own spirituality and return to God; it is called repentance, something modern Christians know little about. May God help us to forsake the world, that we may become the friends of God and no longer His enemies.

3. A third element in approaching God in worship, is the necessity of HAVING A RIGHT CONCEPT OF WHO HE IS.

We must also realize what *we* are and *where* we have come from in relation to God, for a proper perspective.

---

[38] **A.W. Tozer,** <u>The Root of the Righteous</u>

We must see God in the proper perspective of His sinless holiness. We are to be holy in order to come before Him Who is holy.

"[I]t is written, Be ye holy; for I am holy."
— I Peter 1:16

I am going to quote much from the writings of others on this subject. The purpose is to show how we have come to the present state of affairs in this Laodicean Age. I also wish to show what this condition has produced in our churches. I confess that I am just now learning some of these things about worship myself. I think it would better serve the reader to hear from 'old men of God,' from years and centuries past, who we know experienced what I am talking about.

J.C. Ryle, in his classic work on _holiness,_ wrote

"'Sin is the transgression of the law.   — I John 3:4'

"He that wishes to attain right views about Christian holiness must begin by examining the vast and solemn subject of SIN.

➲ He must dig down very low, if he would build high.

"A mistake here is most mischievous. Wrong views about holiness are generally traceable to wrong views about human corruption. I make no apology for beginning this volume of papers about holiness by making some plain statements about SIN.

➲ The plain truth is that a right knowledge of sin lies at the root of all saving Christianity…

"Dim or indistinct views of sin are the origin of most of the errors, heresies and false doctrines of the present day. If a man does not realize the dangerous nature of his soul's disease, you cannot wonder if he is content with false or imperfect remedies. I believe that one of the chief wants of the church in the nineteenth century has been, and is, clearer, fuller teaching about SIN…

"As to the best remedy for the state of things I have mentioned, I shall venture to give an opinion... The cure for evangelical churchmen, I am convinced, is to be found in a clearer apprehension of the nature and sinfulness of SIN... We must simply repent and do our first works. We must return to first principles. We must go back to 'the old paths.' We must sit down humbly in the presence of God, look the whole subject in the face, examine clearly what the Lord Jesus calls SIN, and what the Lord Jesus calls doing His will. We must then try to realize that it is terribly possible to live a careless, easygoing, half-worldly life, and yet at the same time to maintain evangelical principles and call ourselves evangelical people! Once let us see that SIN is far viler and far nearer to us, and sticks more closely to us than we supposed, and we shall be led, I trust and believe, to get nearer to Christ. Once drawn nearer to Christ, we shall drink more deeply out of His 'fullness,' and learn more thoroughly to 'live the life of faith' in Him, as St. Paul did. Once taught to live the life of faith in Jesus, and abiding in Him, we shall bear more fruit, shall find ourselves more strong for duty, more patient in trial, more watchful over our poor weak hearts, and more like our Master in all our little daily ways. Just in proportion as we realize how much Christ has done for us, shall we labor to do much for Christ. Much forgiven, we shall love much. In short, as the apostle says,

'But we all, with open face beholding as in a glass
the glory of the Lord, are changed into the same image,
from glory to glory, even as by the Spirit of the Lord
— II Corinthians 3:18.'" [39]

We must look to the cross of Golgotha (John 19:17), and the immeasurable cost of our redemption if we are to have any understanding of the awfulness of SIN in the eyes of a holy God.

However:

⊃ We shall never have **a right view of His holiness** apart from a right view of the cross.

---

[39] **J.C. Ryle** (1816-1900), Holiness: Its Nature, Hindrances, Difficulties, and Roots

The cross says that our sin is an offense to God and that there is no way to be reconciled to Him apart from the shed blood of "the lamb of God" (Romans 5:10; Colossians 1:21).

➲ We shall never have **a right view of the cross** without a right view of sin.

We must remember that "all our righteousnesses are as filthy rags" (Isaiah 64:6). We must consider the curse of SIN and the judgment of God that must be satisfied.

➲ We shall never have **a right view of SIN** apart from the light of the word of God (John 3:16-21; I Peter 2:9).

We must read the Bible and receive it as the word of God, if it is to work in us (I Thessalonians 2:13).

Here is what the Apostle Paul had to say

"But God forbid that I should glory, save in the cross of our Lord Jesus Christ, by whom the world is crucified unto me, and I unto the world."
— Galatians 6:14

"Giving thanks unto the Father, which hath made us meet to be partakers of the inheritance of the saints in light:

"Who hath delivered us from the power of darkness, and hath translated us into the kingdom of his dear Son:

"In whom we have redemption through his blood, even the forgiveness of sins:

"Who is the image of the invisible God, the firstborn of every creature:

"For by him were all things created, that are in heaven, and that are in earth, visible and invisible, whether they be thrones, or dominions, or principalities, or powers: all things were created by him, and for him:

"And he is before all things, and by him all things consist.

"And he is the head of the body, the church: who is the beginning, the firstborn from the dead; that in all things he might have the preeminence.

"For it pleased the Father that in him should all fulness dwell;

"And, having made peace through the blood of his cross, by him to reconcile all things unto himself; by him, I say, whether they be things in earth, or things in heaven.

"And you, that were sometime alienated and enemies in your mind by wicked works, yet now hath he reconciled

"In the body of his flesh through death, to present you holy and unblameable and unreproveable in his sight:"

— Colossians 1:12-22

Upon Mount Calvary, a holy God and fallen sinful mankind were set in stark contrast, as we were reconciled to the Father by the blood of the cross of Jesus Christ (Colossians 1:14).

We need to return to the "old paths"

"Thus saith the LORD, Stand ye in the ways, and see, and ask for the OLD PATHS, where is the good way, and walk therein, and ye shall find rest for your souls. But they said, We will not walk therein."

— Jeremiah 6:16

Israel KNEW the truth, but they would not walk in the truth. They had developed a *new* way that suited them better. Today, many have said the same thing in their hearts. They know the truth, but will not walk therein. If we would walk in the truth, we must quit worrying about 'feeling good about ourselves' and start worrying about WHY we don't feel bad about ourselves and our sin. We need to glory in the cross of our Lord Jesus Christ and remember that we are crucified with Him (Galatians 6:14; 2:20;

5:24). We are not our own, but we are bought with a price (I Corinthians 6:19-20).

A.W. Tozer said that:

> "We have now raised a whole generation that believes that you can *'accept'* Christ and not forsake the world." [40]

Many years earlier J.C. Ryle (1816-1900) wrote

> "The stream of professing Christianity in this day is far wider than it formerly was, and I am afraid we must admit at the same time it is much less deep... There is a common WORLDLY KIND OF CHRISTIANITY in this day, which many have, and think they have enough— a CHEAP CHRISTIANITY which offends nobody, and requires no sacrifice, which costs nothing, and is worth nothing." [41]

You see, it is nothing new, although it may be packaged a little differently. J.C. Ryle wrote about the condition of the church in the nineteenth century; if the condition of the church was so low then, what is it now. We cannot simply judge ourselves by ourselves (II Corinthians 10:12); we must see ourselves in the light of God's holiness, as set forth in the holy scriptures. Today, many have gone to great lengths to make the Bible and worship appealing to the unsaved and carnal. But this sort of thing is nothing new; it has plagued the Church since its inception. We see the excess and carnal display in the church of Corinth, and for centuries the ceremonies of the Roman Catholic church have appealed to many. But more recently, we have reached an all time low in the excesses of the Charismatic Movement. Now, it has invaded every denomination and even our independent Baptist churches. Worship, and even preaching, have become *entertainment* to many, and our music has become worldly and even devilish. Contemporary songs, blues, bluegrass and even so-called Christian rock music are

[40] **A.W. Tozer**, as quoted by Patrick M. Morley in, The Man in the Mirror: Solving the 24 Problems Men Face (Published by Zondervan, 1997)

[41] **J.C. Ryle**, Holiness: Its Nature, Hindrances, Difficulties, and Roots

now played in *performances* by musicians who have little mind for ministry or God. These are said to be "aids to worship." I suppose when we shut out the Spirit of God, all that remains are these props.

Because we are raising our children in an environment of worship that is anything but holy, we may expect them to fall to even greater depths. See, in the article below, how God is being presented to children today.

From an article, *Sin Is No Laughing Matter*, we read:

"HILARIOUS BIBLE STORIES

"In a recently released movie[42] about the Old Testament story of Jonah, the developers and producers depict Jonah's trip to Nineveh as a 'hilarious showdown.' Hilarious? Sin and wickedness are not 'hilarious.' A prophet defying a command of God is nothing at which to laugh. If a movie presents a serious book of the Bible that deals with sin, repentance, and God's mercy as entertaining and amusing, is the good news of the Bible in danger of becoming the 'fun news' of the Bible?

"Humor is also used in book descriptions to capture the interest of Christian youth. For example, in a book about the 'bad girls' of the Bible, the promotional literature reads:

'[A]n all-new collection of *bad girls* that will tickle your funny bone and challenge you in your spiritual walk.'

"In the contemporary retelling of these biblical stories, is an inaccurate message about the seriousness of sin being inadvertently given? Should sin ever tickle one's funny bone?

"COPYING THE WORLD

"The emphasis on fun and entertainment as a prominent teaching tool is also seen in the popular use of Bible studies that are formatted around TV sitcoms. One can

---

[42] Jonah: A VeggieTales Movie

choose the *I Love Lucy Bible Study;* The *Beverly Hillbillie Bible Study;* or a Bible study based upon the gospel according to Andy Griffith and the town of Mayberry. There is even the *Bart Simpson Bible Study!* For further tickling of the ears, one can even attend a church where the entertainer- preacher known as '*Rockin* Reverend' who, complete with the sideburns, sings like Elvis Presley.

(Agape Press, 01/06/2003)

"SIN IS SERIOUS

"A.W. Tozer identified the escalating trend toward fun and entertainment in the church many years ago, writing:

'And he that taketh not his cross, and followeth after me, is not worthy of me.

'He that findeth his life shall lose it: and he that loseth his life for my sake shall find it.'

— Matthew 10:38-39

'Strange, is it not, that we dare without shame to alter, to modulate the words of Christ while speaking for Christ to the very ones for whom He died?

- Christ calls men to carry a cross; we call them to have fun in His Name.

- He calls them to forsake the world; we assure them that if they but accept Jesus the world is their oyster.

- He calls them to suffer; we call them to enjoy all the bourgeois comforts modern civilization affords.

- He calls them to self-abnegation and death. We call them to spread themselves like green bay trees or perchance even to become stars in a pitiful fifth-rate religious zodiac.

- He calls them to holiness; we call them to a cheap and tawdry happiness that would have been rejected with scorn by the least of the Stoic philosophers.'[43]

"We should be grieved over the sin in our own lives and grieved to see, hear, and read about the sin in others. Our holy righteous God, who is the judge of all with absolute, total power, hates sin, and will burn up with a raging fire all that is not holy. 'Fools mock at sin (Proverbs 14:9), but 'the wages of sin is death' (Romans 6:2).

"Sin creates an impenetrable barrier between us and God. God alone removed this barrier, but its removal was costly requiring the sacrificial death of His Son, Jesus Christ, upon the cross. Yes, God takes sin seriously. Sin is not a laughing matter."[44]

When our children are raised with this view of God, holiness and sin, is it any wonder that their perception of God is warped and their ideas of worship are grossly inadequate? God would have us remember that we are as nothing more than *"the grass"* that *"withereth"* and *"the flower"* that *"fadeth away"* (I Peter 1:24) and our life is but *"a vapour, that appeareth for a little time, and then vanisheth away"* (James 4:14). How then shall we stand before Him, Who is the *"King of kings, and Lord of lords"* (I Timothy 6:15-16). In the Bible, God is highly exalted and man is abased to the dust.

<u>The Bible speaks of the natural man in very unflattering terms.</u>

"What is man, that thou art mindful of him? and the son of man, that thou visitest him?"   — Psalms 8:4

"But I am a worm, and no man; a reproach of men, and despised of the people."   — Psalms 22:6

"The heart is deceitful above all things, and desperately wicked: who can know it?"   — Jeremiah 17:9

---

[43] **A.W. Tozer**, <u>Born After Midnight</u> pp. 141-142

[44] "Sin: No Laughing Matter" From: Youth Ministry Update; www.SpiritualJunkFood.com

"And GOD saw that the wickedness of man was great in the earth, and that every imagination of the thoughts of his heart was only evil continually."

— Genesis 6:5

"Knowest thou not this of old, since man was placed upon earth,

"That the triumphing of the wicked is short, and the joy of the hypocrite but for a moment?

"Though his excellency mount up to the heavens, and his head reach unto the clouds;

"Yet he shall perish for ever like his own dung: they which have seen him shall say, Where is he?"

— Job 20:4-7

By nature we are proud and need to humble ourselves

"Now I Nebuchadnezzar praise and extol and honour the King of heaven, all whose works are truth, and his ways judgment: and those that walk in pride he is able to abase."   — Daniel 4:37

"For whosoever exalteth himself shall be abased; and he that humbleth himself shall be exalted."

— Luke 14:11

"For thus saith the high and lofty One that inhabiteth eternity, whose name is Holy; I dwell in the high and holy place, with him also that is of a contrite and humble spirit, to revive the spirit of the humble, and to revive the heart of the contrite ones."

— Isaiah 57:15

"For all those things hath mine hand made, and all those things have been, saith the LORD: but to this man will I look, even to him that is poor and of a contrite spirit, and trembleth at my word."

— Isaiah 66:2

"The sacrifices of God are a broken spirit: a broken and a contrite heart, O God, thou wilt not despise."

— Psalms 51:17

<u>But God is highly exalted</u>

> "Therefore being by the right hand of God exalted, and having received of the Father the promise of the Holy Ghost, he hath shed forth this, which ye now see and hear."   — Acts 2:33

> "Now unto the King eternal, immortal, invisible, the only wise God, be honour and glory for ever and ever. Amen."   — I Timothy 1:17

> "Wherefore God also hath highly exalted him, and given him a name which is above every name:"
>   — Philippians 2:9

> "The lofty looks of man shall be humbled, and the haughtiness of men shall be bowed down, and the LORD alone shall be exalted in that day."
>   — Isaiah 2:11

> "Thou art worthy, O Lord, to receive glory and honour and power: for thou hast created all things, and for thy pleasure they are and were created."
>   — Revelation 4:11

There was a time when man considered God so lofty and high, and himself so base and sinful, that God seemed almost unapproachable. In these modern times man has elevated himself to such great heights and become so *palsy-walsy* [45] with God, that there no longer seems to be a gulf between the two. God is belittled as "the man upstairs," while man is elevated to be as God. This comes from a lopsided theology that emphasizes some of God's attributes at the expense of others and man's position beyond his rightful place. From the very beginning, Satan has pursued this diabolical strategy.

> "Now the serpent was more subtil than any beast of the field which the LORD God had made. And he said

---

[45] Suggesting a lighthearted, superficial relationship.

unto the woman, YEA, HATH GOD SAID, Ye shall not eat of every tree of the garden?

"And the woman said unto the serpent, We may eat of the fruit of the trees of the garden:

"But of the fruit of the tree which is in the midst of the garden, God hath said, Ye shall not eat of it, neither shall ye touch it, lest ye die.

"And the serpent said unto the woman, YE SHALL NOT SURELY DIE:

"For God doth know that in the day ye eat thereof, then your eyes shall be opened, and YE SHALL BE AS GODS, knowing good and evil."

— Genesis 3:1-5

In the Garden of Eden:

➲ Satan questioned God's word, *"Yea, hath God said?"*

➲ Satan changed God's word, *"Ye shall not eat of every tree of the garden?"*

➲ Satan called God a liar, *"Ye shall not surely die:"*

➲ And finally, Satan suggested to Eve that God was withholding the knowledge of good and evil by which she and Adam could *"be as gods"* themselves.

Today, men worship 'knowledge.' But all knowledge is not truth and knowledge can be twisted and manipulated to the end that man desires. The end of knowledge and the 'sciences' is to make man think he is like God. That is happening today in the realms of science and religion.

Kenneth Copeland is the leading spokesman of the *Word-Faith* movement, which includes such well known personalities as Kenneth Hagin, Benny Hinn and Paul Crouch of Trinity Broadcasting Network (TBN, the so-called "Christian" television network). They teach many heresies, not the least of which is that every born again Christian is a god. You likely will find it hard to believe what you are about to read, but it is true and documented from the original sources.[46]

Kenneth Copeland teaches that:

> "God's reason for creating Adam was His desire to reproduce Himself... and in the Garden of Eden He did just that. [Adam] was not a little like God. He was not almost like God. He was not subordinate to God, even... Adam [was] as much like God as you could get, just the same as Jesus... Adam, in the Garden of Eden, was God manifested in the flesh."[47]

That is blasphemy! None but the Lord Jesus Christ was ever said to be God "manifest in the flesh" (John 1:14; I Timothy 3:16). But, Copeland goes on to say:

> "You don't *have* a 'god' *in* you, you are one."[48,49]

He says Jesus told him:

> "Don't be disturbed when people accuse you of thinking you are God... They crucified Me for claiming I was God. I didn't claim that I was God; I just claimed that I walked

---

[46] "Word-Faith teachers owe their ancestry to groups like Christian Science, Sweden-borgianism, Theosophy, Science of Mind, and New Thought— not to classical Pentecostalism. It reveals that at their very core, Word-Faith teachings are corrupt. Their undeniable derivation is cultish, not Christian. The sad truth is that the gospel proclaimed by the Word-Faith movement is not the gospel of the New Testament. Word-Faith doctrine is a mongrel system, a blend of mysticism, dualism, and gnosticism that borrows generously from the teachings of the metaphysical cults. The Word-Faith movement may be the most dangerous false system that has grown out of the charismatic movement so far, because so many charismatics are unsure of the finality of Scripture (Charismatic Chaos, p. 290)." (From: *Kenneth Copeland: General Teachings/Activities,* by Biblical Discernment Ministries, 1996.) <www.rapidnet.com/~jbeard/bdm/exposes/copeland/general.htm>

[47] **Kenneth Copeland**, Following the Faith of Abraham Part 1, tape 01-3001, side 1, (no date); *Kenneth Copeland Ministries;* From: www.apologeticsindex.org/c53.html

[48] **Kenneth Copeland**, The Force of Love, tape 02-0028, 1987; *Kenneth Copeland Ministries*

[49] *Apologetics Index; Exposing Kenneth Copeland;* www.apologeticsindex.org/c53.html

with Him, and that He was in Me. Hallelujah! That's what you're doing..."[50]

Kenneth Hagin is another of these deluded false prophets of the *Word-Faith* movement who teaches the same wicked lie. He believes that Jesus' incarnation in the flesh was not unique.

Kenneth Hagin says

"Every man who has been born again is an incarnation and Christianity is a miracle. The believer is as much an incarnation as was Jesus of Nazareth."[51]

"'God has made us as much like Himself as possible... He made us the same class of being that He is Himself... Man lived in the realm of God. He lived on terms equal with God... [T]he believer is called *Christ*... That's who we are; we're Christ!'[52]

In exposing such heresy, one preacher writes

"[M]any preachers and teachers... have strayed from the truth... [T]hose who haven't..., don't do much true preaching and teaching. Christianity is continually being watered down, seemingly <u>so it will be *acceptable* even to those outside the Church</u>. It is becoming more saturated with entertainment-based services filled with 'feel-good' theology every day, and most confessing Christians don't even notice, or if they do notice, they don't seem to care...."[53]

The Bible warns us of these dangers

"But there were false prophets also among the people, even as there shall be false teachers among you, who privily shall bring in damnable heresies, even denying the Lord that bought them, and bring upon themselves swift destruction.

---

[50] **Kenneth Copeland**, "Take Time to Pray," *Believer's Voice of Victory*, 2/87, p. 9.

[51] **Kenneth E. Hagin**, The Word of Faith (December 1980) p.13-14

[52] **Kenneth E. Hagin**, Zoe: The God-Kind of Life; (Kenneth Hagin Ministries, 1989) pp. 35-41.

[53] The Bible Page, http://www.thebiblepage.org/about.shtml

"And many shall follow their pernicious ways; by reason of whom the way of truth shall be evil spoken of.

"And through covetousness shall they with feigned words make merchandise of you: whose judgment now of a long time lingereth not, and their damnation slumbereth not."

— II Peter 2:1-3

"If any man teach otherwise, and consent not to wholesome words, even the words of our Lord Jesus Christ, and to the doctrine which is according to godliness;

"He is proud, knowing nothing, but doting about questions and strifes of words, whereof cometh envy, strife, railings, evil surmisings,

"Perverse disputings of men of corrupt minds, and destitute of the truth, supposing that gain is godliness: from such withdraw thyself."

— I Timothy 6:3-5

In the light of verse five, the *Word of Faith* teachings that God wants every man to be rich, and that it is a sin to be poor or sick, are obviously heresy as well. Even many charismatics think these Word of Faith preachers have gone too far.

David Wilkerson said in one of his sermons:

"If you have been feeding your soul on Copeland or Hagin's [teaching], you are not going to like what you hear [in my message today]. Folks I am a shepherd. I've been called by God. I made this church a promise. 'As long as [I am] in this pulpit, if [I] saw wolves in sheep's clothing coming to rob the flock [I] would stand up and cry out against it. It is up to you to do something about it.

"I sat this week and listened to the speakers at this conference and I was so shocked and hurt [that] the burden of the Lord came on me. That is why I am preaching this message. I grieve over it.

"[T]he speakers could hardly get by because all of the people were running up stuffing their pockets with money. The reason they do that is [because of] a new doctrine...

"'If you want to be blessed you have to find the most blessed evangelist or pastor you can..., because he that has been given much receiveth much; he that has little, even that which he has will be taken from him. If you find the most blessed prosperous preacher and give him money, then you will be blessed [in return]...'

"It is a 'pyramid scheme'. If these men were in the secular world, they would be [put] in jail.

"Listen to what... the speaker... said,

"'If a poor widow on welfare hands you $5.00, you better take it. Elijah took the widow's last meal! You are the anointed one, you deserve it, you take it.'

"The same speaker said,

"'I live in a 8,000 square foot house; I am going to build a bigger one now; one that King Solomon would be proud of. I just paid $15,000 for a dog. You see this gorgeous ring on my finger, I was in Jamaica and just paid $32,000 for it. I want you know that when the people in my town come past my mansion and they see my Rolls Royce sitting in the driveway, they know there is a God in heaven.'

"[As your pastor I must warn you]; Don't be deceived by these wicked 'wolves in sheep's clothing!'"[54]

4. A fourth element is THE MANNER OF OUR WORSHIP.

The Bible teaches that we are to worship God "in spirit and in truth" (John 4:23).

When Jesus stopped to talk to the woman at the well, she reflected traditional thinking, but He revealed something more to her.

---

[54] **David Wilkerson**, "The Reproach of the Solemn Assembly" a sermon preached at the Times Square Church, http://truthseekers.8m.com/DOCTRINE/prosperity.html

> "Our fathers worshipped in this mountain; and ye say, that in Jerusalem is the place where men ought to worship.
>
> "Jesus saith unto her, Woman, believe me, the hour cometh, when ye shall neither in this mountain, nor yet at Jerusalem, worship the Father.
>
> "Ye worship ye know not what: we know what we worship: for salvation is of the Jews.
>
> "But the hour cometh, and now is, when the TRUE WORSHIPPERS shall worship the Father in spirit and in truth: for THE FATHER SEEKETH SUCH TO WORSHIP HIM.
>
> "God is a Spirit: and they that worship him must worship him IN SPIRIT AND IN TRUTH."
>
> **— John 4:20-24**

The Lord is interested in 'true worshippers.' Those who do not worship in the proper manner are 'false worshippers.' The woman of Samaria knew that the 'accepted' manner of worship for Jews was only at the temple in Jerusalem. However, (because they were enemies of the Jews), the Samaritans worshipped in their own temple on a mountain in Samaria. But, what this woman did not realize was that after the coming of the Holy Spirit, every believer's 'body' would be the temple of the Holy Spirit. Thereafter, 'true worship' would no longer be restricted to one building or location, but would take place in the heart of any believer, in any place, at any time.

Regarding our manner, we are to worship God "in spirit _and_ in truth.

a. Worship must never be divorced from TRUTH.

It doesn't matter how moving our worship experience may be, our 'experience' must always be subject to scrutiny by the 'truth.' If anything has taken place that contradicts Scripture, it is not 'true worship,' for true worship must be according to _"the word of truth"_ (II Timothy 2:15).

b. And that brings us to the second ingredient of 'true worship.' We must worship "in spirit."

We may worship according to all the word of truth teaches, but still not experience "true worship." We can follow every Bible guideline and every religious tradition perfectly, but it is all in vain if we do not worship in the right spirit.

True worship must originate from within the heart of the worshipper; in the inner man. If we are to worship God, it must take place in our hearts. But, if there are things in our hearts and lives that are unclean or not yielded to His will and authority, then we are not offering true worship to God.

I recently read a sermon that said

"Worship should take place thousands of times before we ever get to this church building. When that is taking place, you don't have to 'gin (work) up' the praise. You don't have to say,

"'All right folks, you weren't singing so hot there. We'll have to crank it up to get you to sing. Come on, now. Somebody surely has something you can thank God for.'

"You don't have to gin that up because you bring the worship with you. It is a corporate service. It is a collection of worship that is taking place everywhere, all week long."[55]

The writer of Psalms says

"This is the day which the LORD hath made; we will rejoice and be glad in it."   — Psalms 118:24

Notice, he says "THE day."

➲ **Doctrinally,** this speaks prophetically of the "Day of the Lord," when Christ shall return to be exalted in His millennial kingdom.

---

[55] Sermon preached at Union Chapel Baptist Church, Marion, Indiana

➲ However, **spiritually,** we may surely apply it to any and every day that we wake and draw breath upon this earth.

If we rejoice in the Lord day by day, it will simply be out of the 'overflowing' joy that we join together to worship corporately at our local church. True 'inward worship' naturally leads to praise, manifested in 'outward worship.'

Remember this and beware

➲ Worshipping in truth, but not in spirit— leads to dead formalism.

➲ Worshipping in spirit, but not in truth— leads to Corinthian type excess like that found in the modern day Charismatic Movement.

We do not want to be guilty of either— we want to have a BALANCE —we want to worship in spirit AND in truth.

c. A third aspect of the manner of our worship is holiness.

"Give unto the LORD the glory due unto his name: bring an offering, and come before him: worship the LORD in the beauty of HOLINESS."

— I Chronicles 16:29

We cannot expect the Lord to accept our worship if we come before Him defiled by the world and unclean. We must present ourselves as vessels made clean and holy. To the degree that we are holy, we are proportionately able to worship God.

There came a time when God would not even accept the sin offerings of the nation of Israel, because their hearts were filled with sin and worldly lusts. Remember, God is 'merciful,' but God is also 'holy.' Even as our prayers may be hindered by our sin, so also may our worship be hindered.

"If I regard iniquity in my heart, the Lord will not hear me:"   — Psalms 66:18

"He that turneth away his ear from hearing the law, even his prayer shall be abomination."
                                        — Proverbs 28:9

"Ye ask, and receive not, because ye ask amiss, that ye may consume it upon your lusts."
                                        — James 4:3

"And Samuel said, Hath the LORD as great delight in burnt offerings and sacrifices, as in obeying the voice of the LORD? Behold, to obey is better than sacrifice, and to hearken than the fat of rams."
                                        — I Samuel 15:22

"I hate, I despise your feast days, and I will not smell in your solemn assemblies.

"Though ye offer me burnt offerings and your meat offerings, I will not accept them: neither will I regard the peace offerings of your fat beasts.

"Take thou away from me the noise of thy songs; for I will not hear the melody of thy viols."
                                        — Amos 5:21-23

"The sacrifice of the wicked is an abomination to the LORD: but the prayer of the upright is his delight."
                                        — Proverbs 15:8

In preparation to worship the Lord we must cleanse and make ourselves holy. We must confess our sins and humble ourselves before the Lord.

"And when he had consulted with the people, he appointed singers unto the LORD, and that should praise the beauty of HOLINESS, as they went out before the army, and to say, Praise the LORD; for his mercy endureth for ever."   — II Chronicles 20:21

"Give unto the LORD the glory due unto his name; worship the LORD in the beauty of HOLINESS."

— Psalms 29:2

"Great is the LORD, and greatly to be praised in the city of our God, in the mountain of his HOLINESS."

— Psalms 48:1

"I speak after the manner of men because of the infirmity of your flesh: for as ye have yielded your members servants to uncleanness and to iniquity unto iniquity; even so now yield your members servants to righteousness unto HOLINESS."

— Romans 6:19

"Having therefore these promises, dearly beloved, let us cleanse ourselves from all filthiness of the flesh and spirit, perfecting HOLINESS in the fear of God."

— II Corinthians 7:1

"For God hath not called us unto uncleanness, but unto HOLINESS."   — I Thessalonians 4:7

J.C. Ryle wrote

"Holiness is the habit of being of one mind with God, according as we find His mind described in Scripture.

"It is the habit of agreeing in God's judgment, hating what He hates, loving what He loves, and measuring everything in this world by the standard of His Word.

"He who most entirely agrees with God, that one is the most holy man."[56]

Andrew Bonar gives us more insight into real worship

"I see plainly that fellowship with God is not 'means to an end,' but is to be the end itself. I am not to use it as a preparation for study or for Sabbath labour, but as my chiefest end, the likest thing to heaven."

"I ought to put into practice in common duties that saying *'Seek ye first the kingdom of God.'* By the grace of God and the strength of His Holy Spirit I desire to lay down the rule…

---

[56] **J.C. Ryle**, Holiness, (Evangelical Press) p.34, ISBN: 0852341369

- Not to speak to man until I have spoken with God,

- Not to do anything with my hand till I have been upon my knees,

- Not to read letters or papers until I have read something of the Holy Scriptures."

All this is but preparation of the heart to worship God. Worship, then, is merely the response of a yielded heart, in thanksgiving to the Lord of Glory, for His mercy and lovingkindness. After preparation through the day comes meditation and devotion at the end.

Andrew Bonar wrote this:

> "I hope also to be able at 'cool of day,' to pray and meditate upon the name of the Lord…"
>
> "In prayer in the wood for some time, having set apart three hours for devotion (worship); felt drawn out much to pray for that peculiar fragrance which believers have about them, who are very much in fellowship with God. It is like an aroma, unseen but felt…" [57]

Holiness brings forth "that peculiar fragrance" that accompanies the manifestation of the fruit of the Holy Spirit in the believer's life.

"For we are unto God a sweet savour of Christ…"
— II Corinthians 2:15

Hezekiah became king of Israel when he was twenty-five years old. The Bible says that "[H]e did that which was right in the sight of the Lord" (II Chronicles 29:2). Under its former king, the nation had fallen into idol worship and the people had forsaken God. Upon becoming king, Hezekiah immediately "[O]pened the doors

---

[57] **Marjory Bonar**, Heavenly Springs (Banner of Truth Trust). Portions of her book were selected from the diary, letters and sermons of her father, Andrew Bonar.

of the house of the Lord..." Then, he called upon the people to repent and ordered that sacrifices be made to atone for their sins.

"And said unto them, Hear me, ye Levites, SANC-TIFY NOW YOURSELVES, and sanctify the house of the LORD God of your fathers, and carry forth the filthiness out of the holy place.

"Moreover Hezekiah the king and the princes commanded the Levites to sing praise unto the LORD with the words of David, and of Asaph the seer. And they sang praises with gladness, and they bowed their heads and WORSHIPPED.

"And Hezekiah rejoiced, and all the people, that GOD HAD PREPARED THE PEOPLE: for the thing was done suddenly.

"Now be ye not stiffnecked, as your fathers were, but YIELD YOURSELVES unto the LORD, and enter into his sanctuary, which he hath sanctified for ever: and serve the LORD your God...

"So there was great joy in Jerusalem: for since the time of Solomon the son of David king of Israel there was not the like in Jerusalem.

"Then the priests the Levites arose and blessed the people: and their voice was heard, and their prayer came up to his holy dwelling place, even unto heaven."

— II Chronicles 29:5, 30, 36; 30:8, 26-27

All this is a beautiful picture of the New Testament believer-priest, preparing his heart and worshipping the Lord today.

Matthew Henry comments on II Chronicles 29:20-36

"(v. 20-36) As soon as Hezekiah heard that the temple was ready, he lost no time. Atonement must be made for the sins of the last reign. It was not enough to lament and forsake those sins; they brought a sin-offering.

- Our repentance and reformation will not obtain pardon but in and through Christ, who was made sin, that is, a sin-offering for us.

"While the offerings were on the altar, the Levites sang.

- (Sorrow for sin must not prevent us from praising God.)

The king and the congregation gave their consent to all that was done.

- It is not enough for us to be WHERE God is worshipped, if we do not ourselves worship with the HEART. And we should offer up our spiritual sacrifices of praise and thanksgiving, and devote ourselves and all we have, as sacrifices, acceptable to the Father only through the Redeemer."[58]

Never can we offer anything to God until we have first offered ourselves (II Corinthians 8:5) in sacrifice to Him. It is but cheap lip service to go to church, sing a few songs, put something in the offering plate and then go back to 'life as usual' the moment we walk out the door. If we have truly worshipped the divine Creator and sustainer of the universe in intimate communion, how could we leave without our lives being truly affected the rest of the day?

---

[58] Matthew Henry's Concise Commentary (Swordsearcher Bible software)

SACRIFICES UNTO THE LORD

Old Testament Sacrifices

Long before the Law was given, Job offered sacrifices to God

"**And it was so, when the days of their feasting were gone about, that Job sent and sanctified them, and rose up early in the morning, and OFFERED BURNT OFFERINGS according to the number of them all: for Job said, It may be that my sons have sinned, and cursed God in their hearts. Thus did Job continually.**"   — Job 1:5

Still before the Law, Abraham and Jacob offered sacrifices

"**And Isaac spake unto Abraham his father, and said, My father: and he said, Here am I, my son. And he said, Behold the fire and the wood: but where is the lamb for a BURNT OFFERING?**"   — Genesis 22:7

"**Then Jacob offered SACRIFICE upon the mount, and called his brethren to eat bread: and they did eat bread, and tarried all night in the mount.**"

— Genesis 31:54

Then, after the Law was given to Moses, and the Aaronic priesthood was established, untold numbers of sacrifices were made before the Lord for the sins of Israel. However important these were, they were but carnal ordinances (Hebrews 9:8-10); they were but a shadow of things to come. The real sacrifices the Lord desired of His people were a broken heart and a consecrated life.

<u>God said to the tribe of Judah</u>

"For I desired mercy, and not sacrifice; and the knowledge of God more than burnt offerings."
— Hosea 6:6

It was God who instituted the sacrifices and burnt offerings. Here, in verse six, He is not telling Hosea that He no longer wanted just those sacrifices. The Lord is saying that what He really desired was for them to see the spiritual meaning in those sacrifices, so as to better understand Who He was.

<u>Below are more examples</u>

"Offer the sacrifices of righteousness, and put your trust in the LORD."   — Psalms 4:5

"The sacrifices of God are a broken spirit: a broken and a contrite heart, O God, thou wilt not despise."
— Psalms 51:17

These sacrifices are seen ever more clearly in the New Testament, after the carnal ordinances are done away with.

New Testament Sacrifices

For the born again believer-priest, there are still other sacrifices that are well pleasing to the Lord.

1. There is a "living sacrifice"

The first spiritual sacrifice we want to look at is found in the book of Romans.[59]

"I beseech you therefore, brethren, by the mercies of God, that ye PRESENT YOUR BODIES A LIVING SACRIFICE, holy, acceptable unto God, which is your reasonable service."   — Romans 12:1

[59] This "living sacrifice" is the same sacrifice we see in Psalm 4:5; 51:17.

Paul beseeches these believers to present their bodies to the Lord.

➲ He instructs them that this sacrifice is **"holy,"** for we are to 'set ourselves apart' for unhindered service unto the Lord.

➲ Furthermore, he says that it is **"acceptable** unto God."

➲ Finally, it is only **"reasonable"** that we make this ultimate sacrifice in His service.

This should not seem an *extraordinary* thing, that would set some Christians above others, but should be the normal service that *every* believer-priest should perform. However, what God considers as no more than "reasonable," many today consider *unreasonable* and more than should be required.

To offer this "living sacrifice" we must die unto SELF (Galatians 2:20) and crucify the FLESH (Galatians 5:24). Sadly, this is appalling to many who are still in love with the pleasures of this WORLD. But, until we can make this first sacrifice, all others are unacceptable. It is one of the keys to true worship.

Romans chapter twelve, verses one and two are often quoted, with little notice of the verses that follow. We ought to be very aware that verses three through eight, that deal with *spiritual gifts* for ministry, are directly related to verses one and two.

Warren Wiersbe says in his New Testament commentary

> "True Christian service and living must begin with personal dedication to the Lord. The Christian who fails in life is the one who has first failed at the altar, refusing to surrender completely to Christ. King Saul failed at the altar (I Samuel 13:8 and 15:10), and it cost him his kingdom.

> "The motive for dedication is love; Paul does not say, 'I command you,' but 'I beseech you, because of what God has already done for you.' We do not serve Christ in order

to receive His mercies, because we already have them (3:21-8:39). We serve Him out of love and appreciation.

"True dedication is the presenting of body, mind, and will to God day by day. It is daily *yielding* the body to Him, having the mind renewed by the Word, and surrendering the will through prayer and obedience... It is only when the believer is thus dedicated to God that he can know God's will for his life...

"As priests, we are to present 'spiritual sacrifices' to God (I Peter 2:5), and the first sacrifice He wants each day is our body, mind, and will in total surrender to Him."[60]

Paul wrote in I Corinthians 15:31 "I die daily."[61] If we, in the same manner, would rise each day and willingly lay ourselves upon the altar like Isaac did, we would be able to face the day victoriously. It is hard to tempt a dead man to sin.

The sacrifice of our own body is not a one time thing, but a *continual* sacrifice that we are to offer day by day, for the glory of God. If we would do this, it would be quite natural for the Holy

---

[60] **Warren Wiersbe**, Wiersbe's Expository Outlines On The New Testament (Victor Books)

[61] A question may arise here about our being "dead in Christ." This problem is resolved in Dr. Peter Ruckman's commentary The Books of First and Second Corinthians— The Bible Believer's Commentary Series, from which I now quote.

"[N]otice there is a 'doctrinal' death and a 'practical' death. In Romans 6:1-6 it is **doctrinal;** you're dead because of your position in Christ. You don't have to '**die daily.'** A dead man can't die daily; he *is* already dead. Romans 6:1-6 is your doctrinal position. That is your **standing**.

Your **state** is that flesh keeps kicking up. Right? All right, then daily you have to die. The practical art is 'mortify therefore your members which are upon the earth;' (Colossians 3:5); 'reckon ye also yourself to be dead; (Romans 6:11), 'die daily' (vs. 31), 'if any man will come after me, let him deny himself, and take up his cross, and follow me' (Matthew 16:24). That's the **practical** position.

Doctrinally you're dead. The Christian is always dead. According to Romans 6, *he is dead and buried with Christ.* According to Colossians 2, he is cut loose from the flesh, and he is still in a corpse, and he carries the corpse until he dies. When you find passages like 'mortify therefore your members which are upon the earth,' that is talking about a *practical* thing. That is talking about *you fighting against the flesh and putting the flesh down.* But as far as the position of your flesh is concerned, *your flesh is dead.*

Spirit to manifest the attributes of Christ by the fruit of the Spirit and to empower us in the exercise of our spiritual gifts.

The Lord Jesus Christ said

> **"And he said to them all, If any man will come after me, let him deny himself, and take up his cross daily, and follow me."**   **— Luke 9:23**

So, among the sacrifices we are to offer unto the Lord, the first one is to deny ourselves and to willingly offer our bodies to His service. Notice Jesus says that each of us has to take up *his own* cross, not Christ's cross. It is not possible that any other but the Lord Jesus Christ could bear the cross that He bore. But the cross is a symbol of death and shame, and of that we must partake if we are to be His disciples.

This is in harmony with the testimony of the apostle Paul

> **"I am crucified with Christ: nevertheless I live; yet not I, but Christ liveth in me: and the life which I now live in the flesh I live by the faith of the Son of God, who loved me, and gave himself for me."**
> **— Galatians 2:20**

Paul, speaking of the churches of Macedonia who gave offerings to meet the needs of the poor saints in Jerusalem, wrote:

> **"And this they did, not as we hoped, but first gave their own selves to the Lord, and unto us by the will of God."**   **— II Corinthians 8:5**

About this "living sacrifice," Albert Barnes says

> "A sacrifice is an offering made to God as an atonement for sin; or any offering made to him and his service as an expression of thanksgiving or homage. It implies, that he who offers it presents it entirely, releases all claim or right to it, and leaves it to be disposed of for the honour of God. In the case of an animal, it was slain, and the blood offered; in the case of any other offering,

as the firstfruits, etc., it was set apart to the service of God; and he who offered it released all claim on it, and submitted it to God, to be disposed of at his will. This is the offering which the apostle entreats the Romans to make; to devote themselves to God, as if they had no longer any claim on themselves; to be disposed of by him; to suffer and bear all that he might appoint; and to promote his honour in any way which he might command. This is the nature of true religion."[62]

A.W. Tozer instructs us further

"The cross stands high above the opinions of men and to that cross all opinions must come at last for judgment. A shallow and worldly leadership would modify the cross to please the entertainment-mad 'saintlings' who will have their fun even within the very sanctuary; but to do so is to court spiritual disaster and risk the anger of the Lamb turned Lion.

"We must do something about the cross, and one of two things only we can do— flee it or die upon it. And if we should be so foolhardy as to flee we shall by that act put away the faith of our fathers and make of Christianity something other than it is. Then we shall have left only the empty language of salvation; the power will depart with our departure from the true cross.

"If we are wise we will do what Jesus did: endure the cross and despise its shame for the joy that is set before us. To do this is to submit the whole pattern of our lives to be destroyed and built again in the power of an endless life. And we shall find that it is more than poetry, more than sweet hymnody and elevated feeling. The cross will cut into our lives where it hurts worst, sparing neither us nor our carefully cultivated reputations. It will defeat us and bring our selfish lives to an end. Only then can we rise in fullness of life to establish a pattern of living wholly new and free and full of good works."[63]

---

[62] Albert Barnes' Notes on the New Testament

[63] **A.W. Tozer**, "The Old Cross and the New," (a pamphlet) paragraph six.

"[It] is going to COST quite a bit... It is never fun carrying a cross. Isn't it strange that Jesus made a bloody, pain-filled cross a symbol of His religion?

"Modern churches have made FUN a symbol of their religion. I want to grieve, bury my head in my hands and sob before God when I hear, as I often do, precious young people whom I would give my blood for, get up and in a little tiny voice say, 'Oh, I am so glad I have found out that you do not have to be a sinner to have fun. We have fun in the church, too. You can follow Jesus and have fun.' Then they sit down. How they have been betrayed! It is the cross that is the symbol of the Christian life. But we will not pick up our cross. We will not forgive our enemies. We will not be reconciled." [64]

The Lord Jesus Christ did not fail to bear the cruel cross of Calvary for us. How then can we faint at bearing our own cross, when we know that we can "[D]o all things through Christ which strengtheneth me" (Philippians 4:13). I am reminded of a lovely old hymn.

MUST JESUS BEAR THE CROSS ALONE?

"Must Jesus bear the cross alone,
And all the world go free?
No, there's a cross for everyone,
And THERE'S A CROSS FOR ME.

"How happy are the saints above,
Who once went sorrowing here!
But now they taste unmingled love,
And joy without a tear.

"The consecrated cross I'll bear
Till death shall set me free;
And then go home my crown to wear,
For there's a crown for me.

---

[64] **A.W. Tozer**, Rut, Rot or Revival

"Upon the crystal pavement down
At Jesus' pierce'd feet,
Joyful I'll cast my golden crown
And His dear Name repeat.

"O precious cross! O glorious crown!
O resurrection day!
When Christ the Lord from Heav'n comes down
And bears my soul away."

Beloved, Heaven will be a sweeter place for them who have willingly borne their cross here on earth. Many look forward to the day they will receive some crown for their works.

But remember!

NO CROSS — NO CROWN

---

2. There is the "Sacrifice of Praise"

The second spiritual sacrifice the New Testament believer-priest has to offer His Lord is found in the book of Hebrews.

After the temple was built in Jerusalem, the Old Testament Levite priests were to "stand every morning to thank and praise the LORD, and likewise at even" (I Chronicles 23:30)

"For by the last words of David the Levites were numbered from twenty years old and above:

"And to stand every morning to thank and praise the LORD, and likewise at even;"

— I Chronicles 23:27,30

It pleased the Lord at the dedication of the temple of Solomon

"Also the Levites which were the singers, all of them of Asaph, of Heman, of Jeduthun, with their

sons and their brethren, being arrayed in white linen, having cymbals and psalteries and harps, stood at the east end of the altar, and with them an hundred and twenty priests sounding with trumpets:)

"It came even to pass, as the trumpeters and singers were as one, to make one sound to be heard in praising and thanking the LORD; and when they lifted up their voice with the trumpets and cymbals and instruments of musick, and praised the LORD, saying, For he is good; for his mercy endureth for ever: that then the house was filled with a cloud, even the house of the LORD;"

— II Chronicles 5:12-13

Today, as believer-priests, we are to offer praise and thanks to the Lord Jesus Christ in all things; this is well pleasing to the Lord.

"Wherefore Jesus also, that he might sanctify the people with his own blood, suffered without the gate.

"Let us go forth therefore unto him without the camp, bearing his reproach.

"For here have we no continuing city, but we seek one to come.

"By him therefore let us offer THE SACRIFICE OF PRAISE to God continually, that is, the fruit of our lips giving THANKS to his name."

— Hebrews 13:11-15

Here, we are reminded of how the Lord Jesus Christ was led *outside* the city to be crucified, because the execution of criminals was not allowed within the walls of Jerusalem itself. On that day, how many of us would have been willing to identify ourselves with Him? How many would have chosen to bear the shame and reproach which He bore? I wonder, if we had been there when He was led away to be crucified, in the midst the angry mocking crowd, would we have stood by His side to be counted as one of His followers? I am afraid that many of us who *profess* to love Him, would have shrunk from following him to Calvary! And many still do. Yes, it is easy to call ourselves *"Christian"* when there is no suffering and reproach. But will we continue to follow Him when persecution comes?

Paul says *"By him... let us offer the sacrifice of praise."* *"By Him,"* as our great High-priest, not by Levite priests upon Jewish altars. The "sacrifice of praise" speaks of the spiritual thank-offering of praise offered to the Lord.

This is what Jeremiah the prophet speaks of

> **"The voice of joy, and the voice of gladness, the voice of the bridegroom, and the voice of the bride, the voice of them that shall say, Praise the LORD of hosts: for the LORD is good; for his mercy endureth for ever: and of them that shall bring the SACRIFICE OF PRAISE into the house of the LORD. For I will cause to return the captivity of the land, as at the first, saith the LORD.   — Jeremiah 33:11**

This is the sacrifice the Psalmist refers to

> **"And now shall mine head be lifted up above mine enemies round about me: therefore will I offer in his tabernacle SACRIFICES OF JOY; I will sing, yea, I will sing PRAISES unto the LORD."   — Psalms 27:6**

> **"I will offer to thee the SACRIFICE OF THANKSGIVING, and will call upon the name of the LORD."**
> **   — Psalms 116:17**

I believe the *"sacrifice* of praise" is more than just normal praise that we offer unto the Lord. From what I understand by the passage of scripture in Hebrews chapter thirteen, it is a *continual* sacrifice that rises as the smoke of incense, a sweetsmelling savor unto the Lord. It issues forth from the soul that identifies with His death; that realizes that the believer is crucified *with* Christ. When we so identify with Him that the altar of His death truly becomes the altar of our death, then the sacrifice of praise may be offered.

Somebody said, "We have to die to our own selves before we can offer the sacrifice of praise." I believe that, and I believe it is especially precious to God, but I wonder how many of us are able to offer this sacrifice when we gather together to worship Him.

Remember when Paul and Silas were imprisoned at Philippi? There, they surely offered the sacrifice of praise when they were in the midst of one of the greatest trials of their lives.

We read the account in the book of Acts

"And at midnight Paul and Silas prayed, and sang praises unto God: and the prisoners heard them."
— Acts 16:25

In my mind, I can imagine Paul now, wishing he had brought a hymnbook. As he and Silas sang and praised the Lord they were much blessed and God was well pleased.

Albert Barnes rightly said

"A Christian may find more true joy in a prison, than the monarch on his throne."[65]

These two apostles were supposed to be in suffering and despair, but instead they were singing and rejoicing. Soon, the pain and discomfort of their wounds, the weight of their shackles and even the darkness of their prison were forgotten, as the Holy Spirit of God ministered unto them while they worshipped the Lord. There was such a movement of God in response to their worship, that the earth quaked and shook the doors open and their bands fell off. They stirred up the other prisoners with their "songs in the night" (Job 35:10) to such a degree that apparently, none tried to escape. The jailor was about to kill himself, rather than be executed for allowing his prisoners to escape, when he heard Paul cry out to assure him they were all still there. When he realized all that had transpired, he fell down before the two preachers and asked "[W]hat must I do to be saved?" What a worship service that must have been!

---

[65] Albert Barnes' Notes on the New Testament

As the Psalmist wrote

> **"They cried unto thee, and were delivered: they trusted in thee, and were not confounded."**
> **— Psalms 22:5**

3. There is the "Sacrifice of Service" [66]

In Hebrews 13:16 we find two more sacrifices

> **"But TO DO GOOD and TO COMMUNICATE forget not: for with such SACRIFICES God is well pleased."   — Hebrews 13:16**

"[T]o do good," in this verse, means "to minister" or "to serve." Just as each Old Testament priest had duties at the house of God, so we all have spiritual duties to attend to.

> **"And above all things have fervent charity among yourselves: for charity shall cover the multitude of sins.**
> **"Use hospitality one to another without grudging.**
> **"As every man hath received the gift, even so MINISTER the same one to another, as good stewards of the manifold grace of God.**
> **"If any man speak, let him speak as the oracles of God; if any man MINISTER, let him do it as of the ability which God giveth: that God in all things may be glorified through Jesus Christ, to whom be praise and dominion for ever and ever. Amen."**
> **— I Peter 4:8-11**

Notice that the exercise of spiritual gifts and ministry (vs. 10) are to be done with "charity" and in the power of the Holy Spirit ("as of the ability which God giveth"). Furthermore, it is to be done according to the word of God, to the end that "God in all things may be glorified through Jesus Christ." All our service is to be done with a right motive or it is in vain. The primary motive in ministering unto others is not simply to give them aid, but to please

---

[66] As regarding our service unto God, refer back to "Ministering Unto the Lord."

God and bring glory to His name. Of course, the only way that can be done is by "charity."

> **"Having then gifts differing according to the grace that is given to us, whether prophecy, let us prophesy according to the proportion of faith;**
>
> **"Or MINISTRY, let us wait on our ministering: or he that teacheth, on teaching;"**
>
> **— Romans 12:6-8**

So, if one has the gift of ministry, one is to "wait on" one's ministering (i.e. "attend to" or "be occupied with" it). Furthermore, while our ministering is often just plain hard work, it should be a labor of love.

> **"For God is not unrighteous to forget your WORK and LABOUR of love, which ye have shewed toward his name, in that ye have ministered to the saints, and do MINISTER."**   **— Hebrews 6:10**

Our service is to be according to the example of Christ, Himself.

> **"Even as the Son of man came not to be ministered unto, but to MINISTER, and to give his life a ransom for many."**   **— Matthew 20:28**

Moreover, the Lord Jesus Christ expects us to minister unto others in the same spirit that we would minister unto Him, "[F]or with such sacrifices God is well pleased."

> **"Then shall he answer them, saying, Verily I say unto you, Inasmuch as ye did it not to one of the least of these, ye did it not to me."**   **— Matthew 25:45**

The providence of God will provide opportunity for us to minister, as well as all that is needed to complete that ministry.

> **"As we have therefore opportunity, let us DO GOOD unto all men, especially unto them who are of the household of faith."**   **— Galatians 6:10**

There is no reason for anyone not to be busy with the Lord's work. There is always service to be done to meet the needs of others.

<u>Albert Barnes comments on Galatians 6:10</u>

"This is the true rule about doing good.

'The opportunity to do good,' says Cotton Mather,[67] 'imposes the obligation to do it.'

"The simple rule is, that we are favoured with the opportunity, and that we have the power. It is not that we are to do it when it is convenient; or when it will advance the interest of a party; or when it may contribute to our fame; the rule is, that we are to do it when we have the opportunity. No matter how often that occurs; no matter how many objects of benevolence are presented— the more the better; no matter how much self-denial it may cost us; no matter how little fame we may get by it; still, if we have the opportunity to do good, we are to do it, and should be thankful for the privilege."[68]

4. There is the "Sacrifice of Giving"

Also from Hebrews 13:16 we learn that there is a sacrifice of giving. (Also see Ministering Unto the Lord)

Paul exhorts his Jewish correspondents to "communicate." By comparing scripture with scripture we learn, from the Bible, the meaning of the word "communicate." Turn in your Bible to Philippians 4:15. There, we see that to "communicate" apparently concerns "giving" (cf. Romans 12:13; Galatians 6:6; I Corinthians 9:7:15). Furthermore, we see that, here too, the "gift," to supply his needs, was a "sacrifice."

"Now ye Philippians know also, that in the beginning of the gospel, when I departed from Macedonia,

---

[67] **Cotton Mather (1663–1728),** was a leading Congregational minister, the most celebrated New England writer of his day and one of the founders of Yale University.

[68] Albert Barnes' Notes On the New Testament

no church COMMUNICATED with me as concerning GIVING and RECEIVING, but ye only.

"For even in Thessalonica ye sent once and again unto my necessity.

"Not because I desire a gift: but I desire fruit that may abound to your account.

"But I have all, and abound: I am full, having received of Epaphroditus the things which were sent from you, an odour of a sweet smell, A SACRIFICE acceptable, wellpleasing to God.

"But my God shall supply all your need according to his riches in glory by Christ Jesus."

— Philippians 4:15-19

This gift was a "sacrifice," that rose up to heaven as "an odour of sweet smell." Not only was it acceptable to God, but wellpleasing. Notice that Paul says, while the gift met his needs, God Himself would, in turn, supply their needs. Furthermore, that supply would be "according to His riches in glory." Once this cycle begins, the exercise of our priesthood connects us to the supply of God and is the source of "many thanksgivings unto God" (II Corinthians 9:12). This supply is according to a spiritual rule that God works by regarding giving. His rule is to supply "abundantly," or, as Paul writes in II Corinthians 9:6 regarding the law of sowing and reaping, "bountifully" (as we have seen earlier under *Ministering Unto the Lord;* cf. Proverbs 3:9-10).

> **"Let your conversation be without covetousness; and be content with such things as ye have: for he hath said, I will never leave thee, nor forsake thee."**
> **— Hebrews 13:5**

Here, "conversation" means "manner of life." We are to live before the Lord and before the world "without covetousness," being content with what we have. "Covetousness" means *"a strong desire after the possession of worldly things"*[69] We read, in

---

[69] Easton's Bible Dictionary

Colossians 3:5, that *"covetousness... is idolatry."* So, our lives are to be characterized by our sacrifice to meet the needs of others, rather than our constant desire for the things of the world. Following are two good examples of the sacrifice of giving.

Remember the story of the woman with the alabaster box?

> **"There came unto him [Jesus] a woman having an alabaster box of very precious ointment, and poured it on his head, as he sat at meat.**
>
> **"But when his disciples saw it, they had indignation, saying, To what purpose is this waste?**
>
> **"For this ointment might have been sold for much, and given to the poor."**
>
> **— Matthew 26:7-9** [70]

Mary broke open a container of fragrant and expensive ointment with which she anointed the body of the Lord Jesus Christ. It was a great sacrifice, for, no doubt, she had purchased it at great price, perhaps even for the anointing of her own body at her burial. The fragrance, not only of the ointment (John 12:3), but of the sacrifice, filled the whole house that day. It was a sacrifice of giving unto the Lord.

The story of another woman's sacrifice is not forgotten either.

> **"And Jesus sat over against the treasury, and beheld how the people cast money into the treasury: and many that were rich cast in much.**

---

[70] **Warren Wiersbie,** Matthew—Be Loyal: New Testament "Be" Series commentaries

"Only John identifies this woman as Mary, sister of Martha and Lazarus. She is found only three times in the Gospels, and in each instance she is at the feet of Jesus. She sat at His feet and listened to the Word (Luke 10:38-42); she came to His feet in sorrow after the death of Lazarus (John 11:28-32); and she worshipped at His feet when she anointed Him with the ointment (John 12:1ff). Mary was a deeply spiritual woman. She found at His feet her blessing, she brought to His feet her burdens, and she gave at His feet her best.

When we combine the Gospel records, we learn that she anointed both His head and His feet, and wiped His feet with her hair. A woman's hair is her glory (I Corinthians 11:15). She surrendered her glory to the Lord and worshipped Him with the precious gift that she brought. It was an act of love and devotion that brought fragrance to the whole house."

"And there came a certain poor widow, and she threw in two mites, which make a farthing.

"And he called unto him his disciples, and saith unto them, Verily I say unto you, That this poor widow hath cast more in, than all they which have cast into the treasury:

"For all they did cast in of their abundance; but she of her want did cast in all that she had, even all her living.

— Mark 12:41-44

As the Bible says

"[T]he LORD seeth not as man seeth; for man looketh on the outward appearance, but the LORD looketh on the heart."   — I Samuel 6:7

So it is with the sacrifice of giving. It is not, at all, how *much* we give, but our heart motive that counts. The poor woman in Mark 12 gave the least of all that day, in the *eyes* of the world. But, in the *eyes* of the Lord she gave more than all; she gave "all that she had." How humbling for those who give much to realize that they have still never given all their living to the Lord. But, if we would ever give all to the Lord, we could surely trust the Lord for all our needs; and the rule for His supply is "abundantly."

As the scripture saith

"There is that scattereth, and yet increaseth; and there is that withholdeth more than is meet, but it tendeth to poverty.

"The liberal soul shall be made fat: and he that watereth shall be watered also himself."

— Proverbs 11:24-25

5. There is the 'Sacrifice of Prayer'

"Let my prayer be set forth before thee as incense; and the lifting up of my hands as the evening sacrifice."   — Psalms 141:2

Here, David likens "prayer" and "the lifting up of... hands" (in prayer), to the sweet incense and sacrifices that were offered every morning and evening within the tabernacle. It seems that prayer, offered as a spiritual sacrifice, involves much more than asking and receiving of the Lord for our carnal needs. Rather, the 'sacrifice of prayer' is an *offering* unto the Lord. It is the type of prayer that requires brokeness of spirit in the one offering it.

<u>Matthew Henry writes</u>

> "Prayer is a spiritual sacrifice; it is the offering up of the soul, and its best affections, to God. ... Those that pray in faith may expect it will please God better than an ox or bullock. David was now banished from God's court, and could not attend the sacrifice and incense, and therefore begs that his prayer might be instead of them.
>
> Note: Prayer is of a sweet-smelling savour to God, as incense, which yet has no savour without fire; nor has prayer without the fire of holy love and fervour."[71]

This typology (prayer as a spiritual sacrifice) is continued in the New Testament. We see, in the book of Revelation, that the prayers of the saints are never lost or forgotten. They continue to be offered as incense, as a sweetsmelling savor, before the Lord.

> **"And when he had taken the book, the four beasts and four and twenty elders fell down before the Lamb, having every one of them harps, and golden vials full of odours, which are the prayers of saints."**
> **— Revelation 5:8**

> **"And the smoke of the incense, which came with the prayers of the saints, ascended up before God out of the angel's hand."**   **— Revelation 8:4**

How many of our own prayers, do you suppose, rise as fragrant incense that is a sweet savor unto the Lord? This type of prayer requires a heart filled with love for God that only comes

---

[71] <u>Matthew Henry's Whole Bible Commentary</u>

from deep meditation upon the person and work of Christ in scripture. We cannot even offer such sacrifice except by the power of the Holy Spirit.

As the Bible says

> **"Then he answered and spake unto me, saying, This is the word of the LORD unto Zerubbabel, saying, <u>Not by might, nor by power, but by my spirit,</u> saith the LORD of hosts."**   **— Zechariah 4:6**

And again Christ saith

> **"I am the vine, ye are the branches: He that abideth in me, and I in him, the same bringeth forth much fruit: for <u>without me ye can do nothing</u>."** **— John 15:5**

It is not the wording of the prayer, but the deep desire for God that motivates our prayers, that are pleasing to the Lord. It is prayer that is fixed on God and hungering and thirsting after *Him*.

It is like the prayer of David in Psalm 42

> **"As the hart panteth after the water brooks, so panteth my soul after thee, O God.**
> **<u>"My soul thirsteth for God</u>, for the living God: when shall I come and appear before God?"**
>   **— Psalms 42:1-2**

Sometimes that desire finds eloquent expression through words, but at other times it is as Paul writes of in his epistle to the Romans; times where no expression can be found in mere words, but only in the groanings of a heart burning with passion for God, Himself.

> **"Likewise the Spirit also helpeth our infirmities: for we know not what we should pray for as we ought: but the Spirit itself maketh intercession for us with groanings which cannot be uttered.**
> **"And he that searcheth the hearts knoweth what is the mind of the Spirit, because he maketh**

intercession for the saints according to the will of
God."

— Romans 8:26-27

King David revealed his heart, at such a time of desire for God

"My heart was hot within me, while I was musing [72]
the fire burned: then spake I with my tongue,"

— Psalms 39:3

Thomas Watson comments [73]

"'[T]he fire burned.' MEDITATE so long till thou findest
thy heart grow warm in this duty. If, when a man is cold
you ask how long he should stand by the fire? sure, till he
be thoroughly warm, and made fit for his work. So, Christian, thy heart is cold; never a day, no, not the hottest day
in summer, but it freezes there; now stand at the fire of
meditation till thou findest thy affections warmed, and
thou art made fit for spiritual service. David MUSED till his
heart waxed hot within him. I will conclude this with that
excellent saying of Bernard:

'Lord, I will never come away from thee without thee.'

"Let this be a Christian's resolution, not to leave off his
meditations of God till he find something of God in him;
some moving of the bowels after God; some flamings of
love (Song of Solomon 5:4).

"Meditation hath a double benefit in it, it pours in and
pours out; first it pours good thoughts into the mind, and
then it pours out those thoughts again into prayer; meditation first furnishes with matter to pray and then it furnishes
with a heart to pray. I was musing, saith David, and the
very next words are a prayer, "Lord, make me to know
mine end." I muse on the works of thy hands, I stretch
forth my hands to thee. The musing of his head made
way for the stretching forth of his hands in prayer. When

---

[72] **musing** v. intr. To be absorbed in one's thoughts; engage in meditation. v.tr. To
consider or say thoughtfully; n. A state of meditation.") American Heritage
Dictionary

[73] **Thomas Watson** was a Puritan divine of the middle to late 1600's.

Christ was upon the Mount, then he prayed: so when the soul is upon the mount of meditation, now it is in tune for prayer. Prayer is the child of meditation: meditation leads the van, and prayer brings up the rear."[74]

Even so, the Psalmist writes

"But his delight is in the law of the LORD; and in his law doth he meditate day and night." — Psalm 1:2

Of this verse, A.W. Tozer comments

"To think God's thoughts requires much prayer. If you do not pray much, you are not thinking God's thoughts. If you do not read your Bible much and often and reverently, you are not thinking God's thoughts..."[75]

In this light, A.P. Gibbs exhorts us regarding *remembrance*

"It is good for the believer to use his memory to recall what he used to be by nature, and what he now is, by God's matchless grace. The words of Paul to the saints at Ephesus are pertinent to this:

'Wherefore REMEMBER that ye being in time past Gentiles in the flesh...

"But now, in Christ Jesus... are made nigh...'
                                            — Ephesians 2:11,13

"Let each Christian call to mind his black past, when he was without God, without Christ, without life and without hope. Then let him contrast this with his present acceptance in the Beloved, together with all the spiritual blessings that are now his present and eternal possession. Surely the result of such remembrance will cause him to lift his heart in adoration to the One who made this so blessedly actual in his experience.

"His memory should also be focused on the Person and work of the Lord Jesus Himself. The purpose of the Lord's supper, as indicated by the Lord Himself is:

---

[74] **C.H. Spurgeon**, The Treasury of David, explanatory notes on Psalm 39:3

[75] **A.W. Tozer**, "Rut, Rot or Revival: The Condition of the Church," from the pamphlet p.42.

'This do in REMEMBRANCE of Me.'   — Luke 22:19

"In view of this, worship will become an essential feature of such a meeting, for *worship is kindled upon the fires of remembrance.* As David puts it:

'While I was musing, the fire burned; then spake I with my tongue.'   — Psalm 39:3

"It is *memory* that enables us to recall the record of His matchless life, as given in the Holy Scripture.

"The Christian should therefore concentrate upon Christ's wondrous words, His mighty deeds, His perfect and holy character, His absolute obedience to the Father's will, His infinite grace in going to the cross, His complete work of redemption accomplished by the sacrifice of Himself, His victorious resurrection, His glorious ascension, and His present ministry as the great high Priest of His people. As he does so, the believer's heart will warm within him, and his worship shall rise to God as a fragrant perfume." [76]

Let us carefully and joyfully fulfill the obligations of our priesthood as believers, giving special attention to the offering of spiritual sacrifices unto our holy God and loving Savior, the Lord Jesus Christ.

---

[76] **A.P. Gibbs**, <u>Worship: The Christian's Highest Occupation</u>, (Walterick Publishers)